POSTMODERN
SOCIAL WORK

POSTMODERN SOCIAL WORK

Reflective Practice and Education

KEN MOFFATT

Columbia University Press   *New York*

Columbia University Press
Publishers Since 1893
New York   Chichester, West Sussex
cup.columbia.edu

Copyright © 2019 Columbia University Press

Library of Congress Cataloging-in-Publication Data
Names: Moffatt, Kenneth James, 1952– author.
Title: Postmodern social work ; reflective practice and education / Ken Moffatt.
Description: New York : Columbia University Press, [2019] |
Includes bibliographical references and index.
Identifiers: LCCN 2019003079 (print) | LCCN 2019004775 (e-book) |
ISBN 9780231549394 (e-book) | ISBN 9780231128001 (hardback) |
ISBN 9780231128018 (trade pbk.)
Subjects: LCSH: Social work education. | Social service—Practice.
Classification: LCC HV11 (e-book) | LCC HV11 .M585 2019 (print) |
DDC 361.3/2—dc23
LC record available at https://lccn.loc.gov/2019003079

Cover design: Elliott S. Cairns
Cover image: *Ocelot* (detail), FASTWÜRMS, 2010.
Oil on canvas, 36 × 48 inches.

CONTENTS

ACKNOWLEDGMENTS

A number of people have been key to the success of this book through their ongoing support and encouragement. I wish to thank Allan Irving, Scott Telek, Sandy McLeod, Patrick deCoste, Keith Cole, R. M. Vaughan, Jennifer Prest, Michael La Sala, Cristina Guadalupe, Nick Dangerfield, Sarah Todd, Lisa Barnoff, Sean Ferkul, and Julian Calleros.

Parts of this book were presented and workshopped at Blue Water Residency, Ontario Canada; Anima Casa Rural, San Isidro Mazatepec, Mexico; and the Doctoral Program at Rutgers University School of Social Work, New Jersey, United States.

POSTMODERN
SOCIAL WORK

INTRODUCTION

Social work education has long been a field in which practitioners theorize ambivalence and change. The comfort level with open process among social work practitioners is more valuable than ever in the contemporary context, which is defined by the speeded-up processes of capitalism and the onslaught of omnipresent technologies. In this book, I explore two broad contemporary interests for social work education. First, I consider a range of influences from technology, neoliberalism, and global capitalism. Second, I discuss the possibilities of a reflective approach to theory and practice. Reflective practice allows one to deal with the shifting landscape that results from constant change while staying true to social work's central concerns. Through reflective practice, social workers can integrate attachment, social welfare, and social justice into direct practice.

This book consists of a series of interlocking essays focused on the theoretical underpinnings of reflective practice in the context of social work education. The book is distinguished by its focus on postmodern theory to elaborate the literature of reflective practice. Each chapter illustrates key postmodern concepts that are relevant to reflection. Throughout the book, my focus shifts between broad social, political, and economic influences and the specifics of personal insight and interpersonal interaction.

Since social work is focused on direct human contact, it is a professional field of practice that is particularly well poised to deal with the continued onslaught of technological and corporate influences in human affairs. Increasingly, technique and technology are central to contemporary communication and the construction of social relationships. Most social interactions are either driven by data or mediated through technology. In addition, social relationships and approaches to social welfare are increasingly imagined through, as well as constrained by, technological forms of communication. An approach to practice that is reflective rather than focused on technically mediated communication allows one to focus on direct experience. Reflective practice also allows one to think about how we make ourselves present in the social context rather than simply responding to external factors such as media and technology.

A strength of the social work field is its focus on the aesthetics of lived experience, which runs counter to technological reductive thinking and abstract generalizations about people. Reductive thinking involves capturing all human processes, no matter how complex, to the smallest measures. Abstract generalization explains phenomena in categories that are meant to be applicable to all human interaction without reference to lived experience and social context. By drawing on the social work practice tradition based in reflection, educators can address the troubling aspects of the rise of reductive and abstract approaches to social welfare by remaining focused on the complexities of process and direct experience. Through a postmodern reflective approach, I hope to make lived experience central to reflection about our pedagogical experiences.

There is a rich literature focused on reflective practice in social work, including clinical and direct practice (Béres, 2014; Béres, Bowles, and Fook, 2011; Fook, 2016; Fook and Askeland, 2007; Fook and Kellehear, 2010; Hyatt, 2014; Mandell, 2007; Miehls and Moffatt, 2000), community practice work (Barnoff and Moffatt, 2007; Burstow, 1991; Harms Smith and Nathane-Taulela, 2015; Lee, 1999; Lee, McGrath, Moffatt, and George, 2002; Moffatt, U. George, Lee, and McGrath, 2005; Parada, Barnoff, Moffatt, and Homan, 2010; Willson, 2018), postmodern approaches to reflection (Béres, 2012; Chambon, 1994, 1999; Donovan, Rose, and Connolly, 2017; Healy, 2005; Healy and Leonard, 2000; Irving, 1994, 1999, 2014; Irving and Young, 2002, Morley, 2014; Phillips, 2007; Ungar, 2004), arts-based reflection (Barnes, 2015; Chambon and Irving, 2003; R. Jackson, Debassige, Masching, and Whitebread, 2015; Moffatt, 2012a; Paton, 2015; Sinding and Barnes, 2015; Trevelyan, Crath, and Chambon, 2012; Wehbi, 2015; Wehbi, McCormick, and Angelucci, 2016; Wehbi, Preston, and Moffatt, 2016; Wilson et al., 2016), critical approaches to reflection (Fook, 2016; Heron, 2005; Martinez-Brawley, 2001; Martinez-Brawley and Zorita, 2007), and social-constructionist reflective approaches (Fook, 2014; Gardner, 2012; M. Keenan, 2012; Kumsa, 2012; Witkin, 2012a, 2014b).

Reflective social work practice defies simple categorization since reflection involves complexity. For example, the work of Irving (1999, 2014) is not easily contained within the categories of postmodern, social-constructionist, or arts-based approaches to social work knowledge and practice. Barnes (2015) approaches reflective practice in a manner that includes direct practice,

3

community practice, and arts-based approaches. R. Jackson et al. (2015) build on narrative reflexivity as a form of culture building, as well as a method to discuss colonization, indigenous knowledge, and the arts. I build on this strong interdisciplinary social work literature to discuss reflection in the postsecondary social work classroom and to think through practice approaches.

Postmodern social work invites us to rethink the traditional social work categories of clinical, community, and policy practice. Instead, postmodern frames of reference for social work allow one to explore concepts of practice that defy categories based on level of practice. For example, concepts such as self, power, discourse, subjectivity, consciousness, affect, and emotions are both individual and social in nature. Throughout the book, I provide a conceptual postmodern frame for reflective practice by elaborating on concepts such as self, power, discourse, *history of the present,* tacit knowledge, *psychic space, subject in process,* ascesis, the planar, *assemblage,* and *rhizomatic change.* Philosophers I draw on in the book include Zygmunt Bauman, Judith Butler, Michel Foucault, Julia Kristeva, Gilles Deleuze, and Félix Guattari, who are loosely grouped in the canon of postmodernism.

As I was writing the book, the work of Deleuze and Guattari (1983, 1987) led me to reconsider my presence in my narratives about the classroom and influenced my approach to the book. Educators too often anticipate and define the desires of our students. This representation of student desire often unintentionally serves to disrupt its expression. By capturing student desire conceptually, educators might also inadvertently serve the purposes of capitalism (Deleuze and Guattari, 1983). This type of thought has also helped me think about the elusive qualities of practice, such as a desire for attachment and a desire to help, alongside the pragmatics of practice.

Deleuze and Guattari (1983) discuss how the representation and coding of desire are a disruption of and containment of its expression. They "valorize an economy of desire" (Dosse, 2010, 211) and remind us of the significance of affect and drive. In other words, the subjective involvement of students is an "economy of desire." Desire or subjective engagement makes possible a series of arrangements that are multiple and, at times, elusive (Dosse, 2010, 220). Respecting this mode of existence involves giving preference to the economy of desire over the "formal logic of the signifying chain" (Dosse, 2010, 211). In other words, the interpretation that the professor provides about students' desire by recounting their experience begins the process of the signifying chain. To avoid the risk of constructing and reconstructing student desire and containing it through my own thought process, I have disrupted my reporting of the tacit knowledge in the classroom. As much as possible, I have avoided reporting specific interactions with students. The educator's report from the classroom too often becomes a narrative about teaching successes or situations in which the enlightenment of the professor guides students through thorny problems.

In the past, I felt my observation of student engagement was a helpful resource, but now I believe my commentary on specific engagements is a type of overcoding. This type of discussion of students in the neoliberal, capitalist university acts as a type of coding of desire (see Deleuze and Guattari, 1983, 1987). Such a commentary suggests I know what students should feel and think, as well as how they should combine affect, emotions, and cognitive thought. In a contemporary technology-driven context, such a process is too close to data mining, whereby emotions, thought, and behavior become data for research and surveillance. So, instead of discussing the reactions of students, I focus on the methods I use to measure student involvement in order to illustrate how I activate some of my ideas. In a break from the past, I focus more on the teaching modalities that I introduce to classroom learning than on specific classroom interactions. These methods, of course, are then open for discussion and reflection.

I am aware of my role as an educator who influences student engagement, draws on personal subjectivity, and acts a representative of a neoliberal institution. In these multiple roles, I create symbols and codes about students, including grades, that may inadvertently be taken up for capitalist consumption. Since these roles are often in tension and need to be thought through, it makes sense to take a reflective approach to education and practice. Throughout the book, I intersperse reflections on ways in which I have attempted to make the concepts actionable or operational through exercises and pedagogical approaches. Most of these methodologies are not necessarily new, but I hope that the manner in which I consider them theoretically sheds a new light on our approaches to education.

OUTLINE OF THE BOOK

Chapter 1 outlines the broad, socioeconomic context of the social work classroom. This chapter draws on the thought of Bauman, Butler, and Foucault. It begins with an outline of a Foucauldian approach to understanding power, strategic power relations, and discourse. The combination of power and discourse constructs reality rather than defining reality, leading to the possibilities of the constitution of the self. By conceptualizing the classroom as the focal point, I engage in a *history of the present*. The classroom is thought of as a web of strategies of power and relationships that reflect but do not wholly replicate broader social relationships. I make the case that we face two troubling social changes in the contemporary context: the reactionary attempt to define knowledge through certitude, on the one hand, and, on the other hand, the increasing precariousness of social life. I argue that, currently, the three discursive frameworks of neoliberalism, new managerialism, and technology make truth claims that are tied to control. These discourses are thus constructed in a manner that obscures precariousness. I argue for a postmodern approach to reflection that can deal with ambivalence and change and that questions the nature of truth. I ultimately argue that educators should face ambivalence, multiplicity, and precariousness to help students understand social welfare and health in the contemporary context.

In chapter 2, I discuss reflective approaches, with a focus on social work education. I begin by discussing Donald Schön's work on reflective professional practice. I then argue that social work literature enriches Schön's approach to reflective practice. Social work theorists demand more of the practitioner by developing critical reflective approaches that focus both on the social context of practice and on changing the self of the practitioner. In this manner, social work theorists correct for a tendency to treat Schön's thought as a technical exercise in professional problem solving. The special quality of social work literature on reflective practice involves this careful consideration of the practitioner's self. Finally, I argue that social work reflective-practice literature has a particular strength because of its supple approach to social justice.

In chapter 3, I focus on reflective practice as a form of consciousness. I begin with social-constructionist approaches to social work that are the basis for discussing how we make the self present in the classroom. I then discuss Paulo Freire's influential work on reflective community practice, and I draw on the work of Kristeva to outline a contemporary approach to the development of consciousness that takes into consideration the problem of image saturation in a contemporary consumerist society. Kristeva argues for an approach to reflection that allows identity to be open and shifting while taking into consideration the importance of symbol creation. Her concepts of *psychic space* and the *subject in process* are useful to social work educators who take an approach to reflective learning that asks students to engage in personal and social change. I provide an example of how I attempted to help students work through engagement in psychic space and the subject in process.

I discuss the classroom as a play of dynamic elements in chapter 4. I push the limits of my own understanding of the diversity within the classroom by considering the thought of Deleuze and Guattari. Basic concepts about the selves of the student and the educator are challenged through these authors' concept of *assemblage*. Assemblage, which includes both human and nonhuman elements, exists outside the embodied self. I critically reflect on my past teaching practices, which involved the expectation that students make identity claims in the classroom. I trouble my assumption that encouraging this type of speaking about the self necessarily leads to a type of empowerment through voice. I broaden the components or elements of the class that we need to reflect on as educators by outlining key concepts associated with Deleuze and Guattari, including the *planar*, *assemblage*, and *rhizomatic change*. I then discuss my attempt to create assignments in a queer theory class that are attentive to the possibility of rhizomatic change. In chapter 5, I focus on the construction of the educator as a *dispossessed self.* By focusing on myself, I argue that the construction of gender, particularly masculinity, and race, particularly whiteness, must be reflected on. I then outline a transformation of the reflexive self that involves moving from psychodynamic practitioners' preoccupation with homeostasis and toward becoming open to the other. Drawing on the thought of Butler, I enrich the concept of the reflexive self by considering the idea of the dispossessed self. Through this form of reflexivity, I imagine a type of radical openness to the other (the students) that results in a *coming undone* of the educator. I reflect on some of the consequences for classroom educational processes if we take this approach to our presence as educators.

In chapter 6, I argue, based on my discussion of affect and emotions, for an arts-based interdisciplinary approach to social work that includes both emotional and cognitive content. An art-based social work practice allows for reflection on how we reveal the self in the classroom, as well as the essential component of emotions in personal and social change. Furthermore, I argue that as educators we need to develop, through reflective practice, a literacy of commercial imagery.

In chapter 7, I outline some of the key elements of reflective social work practice in education that are informed by postmodern theory. I discuss some of the key concepts related to reflective practice that the book examines. These include postmodern reflection on the creation of meaning and knowledge, using reflection as a means to trouble discourse, and making one's self present as a process that is never ending and tentative, as well as effecting psychic change through reflection.

SOME KEY THEMES

Reflection

The central theme of the book is reflective practice, and my intent in writing it was to elaborate on that practice. The book provides a survey and critical review of the widely used approaches to reflection developed by Schön and Freire. I advance reflective theory and practice by drawing on postmodern thinkers to elaborate on concepts in order to think about reflective practice. I take time to outline the work of Jan Fook, who has been influential in developing reflective practice in the fields of social work and health care. I also draw on the rich body of social work literature focused on reflection.

One of the ways to adapt to the difficult and rapidly changing social environment in which we live is through reflective thought. The reflective approach to practice allows us to reconsider the increasing precariousness, insecurity, and fragmentation of social life by continuously reconsidering one's own influence and the construction of oneself as a social agent.

Reflection also helps one think through the relations of inclusion and exclusion that lead to silence or the absence of some voices. The postmodern approach to social work reveals and troubles the many manifestations of power. Power is present at all times in strategic relations, but these relations of power can be deconstructed and reconstructed through reflection on thought and practice.

As educators, practitioners, and students, we make ourselves present in the context of social relations. Through reflective practice, we can consider the social relations that construct the self in both dangerous and welcoming ways. Reflective practice allows one to experiment with expressions of the self that are not yet fully imagined or that have been socially constrained. In addition, reflective practice helps a student or professor to reconcile the multiple expressions of the self.

In this book, I am interested in reflective practice that includes some of the more elusive elements of social engagement, such as affect, emotions, and consciousness. Reflection also allows one to engage in a multidimensional process that includes affect, cognition, process, and practice. Rather than think of the classroom as a unitary entity, I reflect on the multiple components in the classroom that influence our approach to and engagement in the classroom.

Precariousness

As I began to think through reflection, I became aware of how precariousness is a social condition and a condition of the self that can be addressed through the practice of reflection in the contemporary context. Too often, the discourses of neoliberalism, new managerialism, and technology are drawn on as if they have a universal application that leads to a sense of stability and security. Instead, these discourses have had the paradoxical consequence of increasing precariousness in social and economic well-being. Acknowledging social precariousness and the attendant lack of certainty is the first step in defining how to act in a socially responsible manner.

Social precariousness is felt through a number of factors, such as economic inequality, prejudicial relationships, violent acts of the state, restructuring of the workforce, and random violence. Precariousness is so widespread that it is palpable to all, but there is a concerted effort to avoid facing it. Reflective practice is a mode to work through a fragmented and inequitable social context in which people are too often imagined to be autonomous.

Precariousness happens at the broadest social level but also in our construction of ourselves. Social workers can contribute to understanding psychosocial dynamics through ambivalent thought in a precarious time. Furthermore, I outline how the type of personal and social change that we ask of students in the classroom can lead to a feeling of rootlessness and precariousness among students. I ultimately argue for a self that is open to precariousness that is experienced as *coming undone*.

The Self

Throughout the book, I explore concepts of the self in social work literature while reconsidering and enriching them by referring to postmodern theory. The self is conceptualized as a social phenomenon that is made possible and constrained by social relationships. It is constituted through the matrix of discourse, knowledge, power, and relationships. Social work, with its interest in concrete human relations, is a discipline that is well suited to helping practitioners think about and reflect on the aesthetics of the self. Making oneself present in the social world is what Foucault refers to as the aesthetics of the self, or *ascesis*. While I still am attached to and interested in the possibility of a "realized" or fully developed self, I am also interested in the possible dissolution of the self as we know it as a way to promote social change.

Technology

Technology is explored throughout the book in a variety of forms. The need to deal with technology is tied to its omnipresence, as well as its taken-for-granted social context, which emerges from its development as a "necessary" goal of productivity. Technology is reflected on as a way of thinking or a discursive frame both historically and today. I outline the discourse of technique or technology during the early years of the social work profession. I also outline the nature of a technological approach to development in the contemporary context. Schön discusses the limits of a technological or scientistic reductive approach to practice in his critique of technical rationality. Furthermore, I discuss technology as a mode of delivery for education, as well as a factor in classroom dynamics. Finally, technology has made possible the spread of images that act as normative discourses tied to global commercialism and capitalist competition. Reflection can aide in social work meaning making by addressing the troubling decontextualized images associated with media and the collapsing meaning of identity because of technology. Meaning making is also enhanced by focusing on nonmediated direct practice that is not filtered through the lens of technology. At times, finding a quiet space, a space of reflection, may be the best way to reflect on the self in the context of disruptive technologies.

1

DISCOURSE IN THE CONTEXT
OF PRECARIOUSNESS

I have taught general courses for graduate programs at two American and two Canadian universities. These courses focused on questions of knowledge construction, the marginalization of communities, identity formation, and systems of control as they pertain to the profession of social work. Each time I teach one of these required courses, major global events remind me and the students that we are in a time of instability and social risk. In fact, at times, it is easy for me to imagine that the global economic and social systems are in collapse. I perhaps felt this most urgently when I was teaching at Smith College the summer after the attack on the World Trade Center on September 11, 2001. Recent social, economic, and political changes, such as the election of President Donald Trump and politicians like him and the attack on social security systems across North America, have caused social work classes to occur, once again, in a context of extreme social risk. Today in both the Americas and Europe, the withdrawal of support from the most marginalized is coupled with a reimagining of social, national, racial, political, and economics boundaries so far reaching that no one knows the nature of the future of social relationships. This is coupled with a turn toward a provincial approach to nation-states whereby people protect their economic interests by blaming the so-called infiltration of refugees and immigrants.

Capitalist change is based on the unequal distribution of both risk and security among populations. Each time I teach these courses, I feel that the field of social work, and the other caring professions, is more necessary than ever to promote an articulate, critical, and reasonable approach to social change. The precariousness and risk associated with contemporary social political realities call for a critical approach to social work that intricately combines personal well-being and socioeconomic change. Furthermore, a body of social work knowledge is needed to help us better understand the nature and experience of vulnerability, marginalization, colonialism, and exploitation in the face of the forces of global change.

At the same time, the profession of social work can position itself to remind us of the moral imperative to address the rise of precariousness and its unequal distribution. This awareness of precariousness, and knowledge about how to take action to remedy social inequity, can act as a foundation for contemporary social work. Furthermore, the caring professions, if carefully considered, can contribute to providing a voice in support of those people who are most marginalized by economic and social forces. Because of the constant change in social circumstances and the persistence of the sense of risk and precariousness within the social body, a reflective approach to practice offers a frame for understanding, ethical interpretation, and action.

The history of North American social work practice and social welfare policy includes a large number of historical initiatives to enhance social well-being. The approaches may be divided into those that have sought social stability and control and those that are more open-ended in the interpretation of personal and social well-being. Often, attempts at social improvement and social control have been based in idealism and the attempt to create a more equitable social order (Moffatt, 2001a). Social work professionals and theorists have been preoccupied with improving the moral order (Gibson, 2015; Moffatt, 2001a; Valverde, 1991), facilitating the integration and assimilation of marginalized people and immigrants (Moffatt, 2001a), and providing social protection against risk (Moffatt, 2001a; Rose, 1999; Rose, O'Malley, and Valverde, 2006). Unfortunately, these attempts by social workers to contribute to social order and stability have resulted in some troubling colonial relations between Indigenous persons, marginalized populations, and social workers (Gibson, 2015; Gosine and Pon, 2011; R. Jackson et al., 2015; Moffatt, 2001a; Pon, Gosine, and Phillips, 2011).

Another historical approach to social work has been constructed through interdisciplinary thought, with a focus on openness of thought and practice skill, in the face of complexity and ambiguity (Hyatt, 2014, Hyatt and Good, 2017; Irving, 1994; Martinez-Brawley and Zorita, 2007; Moffatt, 2001a; Sinding and Barnes, 2015). In light of the long historical stretch of social and economic turbulence arising from capitalism (Bauman, 2012), I am interested in this open approach to social work, and specifically in the question, How do social work knowledge and practice deal with uncertainty, tenuousness, and *not knowing?*

In this chapter, I argue that social work educators should teach about risk and precariousness rather than rushing to a discussion of stability. I begin the chapter by introducing Michel Foucault's concepts of power, the discursive construction of the self, and the *history of the present* in order to think through how educational discourses are constructed in contemporary postsecondary institutions. I outline three contemporary conceptual frames or discursive practices that I believe constrain how we think about social practice, social processes, and social change. Each of these discursive frames attempts to introduce a sense of certainty to social practices. These discourses include neoliberalism, new managerialism, and a technological worldview. I then discuss the aversion to precariousness in contemporary discourse and how this contributes to marginalized people being lost in the historical record. I outline some of the tenets of the postmodern approach to social work as a theoretical frame that is congruent with and can address the contemporary social context. Finally, I discuss the implications for reflective teaching while offering an example of a teaching method that attempts to redress the silence of student voices in the contemporary classroom.

A FOUCAULDIAN APPROACH: POWER, DISCOURSE, AND CONSTITUTION OF THE SELF

I tend to teach survey courses focused on the social context of practice at the graduate level. In those courses, my teaching approach has been to define contemporary social relationships in order to imagine how they affect our roles and identities as professors and students. Rather than take a structural approach to education that defines large social structures that create inequity outside the classroom and that assumes all economic relations necessarily and directly influence the nature of professional education (Mullaly, 2007), I take an approach based on Foucault's analysis. I argue that while broader frameworks about social and economic relations affect postsecondary education, the classroom experience is complicated through the introduction of multiple discursive regimes. These regimes constrain our thinking about postsecondary education and, at times, discipline and restrict our educational practices. At the same time, discourse is not only about constraint; it also defines who we are in the classroom in both productive and troubling ways (Sirotich, Martin, Ruhinda, Vaz, and Moffatt, 2012).

Power

According to Foucault (1988b), power is a type of relation that exists between individuals. Power is not a principle of individual character, an unfathomable property, or a substance one possesses. Instead, every relationship is also a relationship of power (Foucault, 1988b). Power relations are inherently neither good nor bad, but each is dangerous (Foucault, 1980c; Gordon, 1980; Kritzman, 1988; Moffatt, 1999a).

In addition, power is multiple and strategic (Foucault, 1979). In a broader context, it is the complex strategy of relations within a society (Foucault, 1980c). It is distributed widely rather than concentrated solely at points of privilege. In the contemporary context, the operation of power exists "everywhere in a continuous way" (Foucault, 1979, 80). It is constant, regular, and very specific in its effects. This form of power is advantageous to those in control who wish to induce social order because it can be induced in the smallest element of the social body, including at the point of microinterventions (Moffatt, 1999a). Historically, the exercise of power has become more efficient and less

19

wasteful now that it is exercised widely and continuously. Economic and political costs are minimized by the increased strategic use of power, and its effectiveness has been enhanced (Foucault, 1979; Foucault, 1980a). For example, social workers utilize power when intervening with their clients through assessment and surveillance. This exercise of power among many workers distributes the power widely to avoid costly mechanisms of central control (Moffatt, 1999a).

Foucault's understanding of power helps us to understand how power is both exercised and experienced. When we understand that power is exercised, we can conceptualize power as if it is both repressive and productive. It is not always imposed from hierarchical centralized structures but also comes from the "bottom up" (Fook, 2016; Healy, 2000; Wang, 1999). Because power does not exist in a substantive form, neither does it exist as a separate form at the level of the institution or the social structure (Gordon, 1980). Since power is a factor of social relationships, it is not finite in nature. Power is used by different people in differing settings. So the context influences the strategies of power, as well as how they are used by people (Baldwin, 2004; Fook, 2016; N. Gould, 2004; N. Gould and Baldwin, 2004; Healy, 2000).

Discourse and the Self

At the same time, power is intricately linked to networks of signs and language or discourse. According to Foucault (1997b), these discourses, made up of technologies of sign systems and linguistic forms, do not simply describe reality; rather, they create reality (Chambon, 1999; Foucault, 1972; Irving, 1994; Sirotich et al.,

2012). It is through discourse that we explain, characterize, and name our reality, but, more importantly, it is through discourse that we shape it (Chambon, 1999; Fook, 2016; Foucault, 1997b). The reality shaped by discourse both exists in the moment it is constituted or spoken and is sustained over time. Each of us is subject to discursive regimes that are related to systems of power (Foucault, 1972).

At any historical moment, discourses define the knowledge and expressions of the self that are legitimate. It is these discursive regimes that regulate how we engage in the social world and therefore constitute ourselves. Dominant discourses are influential in the constitution of subjects through the repetition of practice (Chambon, 1999; Irving, 1994, 1999; Trevelyan et al., 2012). Discourses affect not only subjectivity or the understanding of the self but also the possibility of expressing the self, since discourse is understood to be "a system of representation that establishes what selves are conceivable" (Trevelyan et al., 11).

Foucault's History of the Present

Foucault's approach to historical forces allows us to consider the specific mechanisms of power as they play out in institutional contexts. Foucault sought to understand how the present is constituted through knowledge claims and discursive regimes. His interrogation of the present seeks to reveal the relationship between truth, the subject, and how experience is constituted (Foucault, 1980a, 1980b). For example, through his archival research of the French prison system, he explored how power is manifested as part of a *history of the present*. He was particularly interested in how power and knowledge are deployed for

21

exercises in subjection and discipline. Furthermore, he noted that a tangle of economic, juridical, and psychiatric concepts acts as a veil over certain voices in the archives, such as those of the prisoners who are most affected by these practices and concepts, making it difficult to hear their unmediated voices and better comprehend their ways of understanding (Foucault, 1979).

At times, discursive regimes and generalized patterns of thinking can be countered through specific inquiries. Not only was Foucault interested in how social relations were constituted, but he was equally interested in how we might promote change by discovering and promoting lines of fragility within truth claims and the constitution of experience (Foucault, 1988a, 37). Foucault (1988a) formed a line of inquiry that reveals exclusions and silences in social structures and epistemological frameworks.

The history of the present is a method that allows us to reflect on our educational programs, as well as the manner in which we teach, in the context of precarious global relationships. By looking for discursive forms that influence our ways of knowing, we can explore the complexity of differing social demands on the classroom. By understanding how the expression of the self is constrained by language and symbol, we can reflect on the conflicting demands on subjectivity in the classroom. Through an analysis of the history of the present, we can look for fractures and cracks in the dominant discursive practices. We can also engage in strategic work to encourage the expression of productive power among students who have felt constrained by disciplinary educational mechanisms.

Historian and philosopher Didier Eribon (1991) shares the contents of a 48-page booklet titled *Intolerable 1*, written in 1971 for Group D'Information sur les Prisons. In this booklet, Foucault outlines a methodology to study institutions—in this case, the French prisons—in order to reveal practices of inclusion and exclusion. Foucault, in his interest to deconstruct institutional power relations, wrote in 1971: "These investigations are not intended to ameliorate, alleviate, or make an oppressive system more bearable. They are intended to attack it in places where it is called something else—justice, technique, knowledge, objectivity. Each investigation must therefore be a political act" (Foucault cited in Eribon, 1991, 228). Furthermore, according to Foucault,

> These investigations are not made from the outside by a group of technicians. Here the investigators and investigated are the same. It is up to them to speak, to dismantle this compartmentalization, to formulate what is intolerable and to tolerate it no longer. It's up to them to take charge of the struggle that will prevent the exercise of oppression. (Foucault cited in Eribon, 1991, 228)

While the many mechanisms of the politics of inclusion and exclusion in the classroom act in conformity with the power of administration, through this approach one does not simply interrogate the social system as a whole for its structures of exclusion. Rather, the investigator questions the ensemble of acts, policies, and instruments put in place through the institution of the university and in the classroom (Eribon, 1991). The history of the present allows the educator to work along with students to become aware, to document, and to change troubling social interactions.

Educators can question the range of acts, as well as the range of concepts, that limit our thought. The analysis of educational settings from a Foucauldian point of view acknowledges that both students and professors are caught in a network of policy provocations or systems of governance. The obfuscation of voices that Foucault studied in the French penal system continues to this day through a multitude of contemporary institutions, including universities, hospitals, and social service agencies (Eribon, 1991).

I teach reflectively from an approach that is based in the thought of Foucault. As a teaching method, I make visible, to the best of my ability, the concepts and mechanisms of governance that constrain both the students' and the professors' thought. At the same time, I encourage a process of reflection among the students to help find voice within and resistance to these discursive structures. The students and professors interested in social change reflect on those lines of fragility that allow for a method of getting outside the taken-for-granted truth production in the university. The students and I imagine how to make visible taken-for-granted discourses so that they are open to critical reflection. I also introduce the discourses of people whose subjectivities are not supported in the classroom in order to begin a process of imagining anew our social relations. In the next section, I outline some discursive structures, or *epistemes*, that govern thought and practices in the postsecondary educational system. These discourses are part of the aforementioned tangle of economic, juridical, and governing concepts that construct possibility in our classrooms. These discourses define the practices and possibilities in the classroom, or, in other words, create our reality. The role of these discourses is to allude to certitude in our contemporary social context, which is in fact characterized by risk and precariousness.

CONTEMPORARY DISCURSIVE REGIMES

In *The Order of Things*, Foucault argues that in any culture there is an episteme that defines the conditions that make knowledge possible. Foucault (1972) defines *episteme* as a type of worldview. The episteme, according to Foucault, is "the total set of relations that unite, at a given period, the discursive practices that give rise to epistemological figures, sciences, and possibly formalized systems" (Foucault 1972, 191). According to Irving, the episteme is "the conditions of the possibility of thought in a given historical period, legislating and establishing the limits of understanding" (1999, 36). The episteme is not necessarily expressed through theory or defined as a concrete practice (Foucault, 1972).

It is my contention that the episteme of our time is the structure of concepts that suggests that permanent and definitive social structures exist. In an attempt to deal with social precariousness, discursive structures are constructed and then proved through reference to "stable," empirical fact. I outline three discursive regimes that contribute to this overall episteme: neoliberalism, new managerialism, and a technological worldview. This discursive framework becomes a lens through which we can understand struggles over knowledge in social work, as well as how discourses contribute to the nature of social relations (Moffatt, 2001a).

Neoliberalism

For decades, neoliberal ideology and regulation have been shaping North American university education, as well as the actors within colleges and universities (Davies, 2005; Deem, 2008;

Deem, Hillyard, and Reed, 2007; Farrell and Morris, 2003; Todd et al., 2015; Todd et al., 2017). In a broad sense, *neoliberalism* refers to the subordination of all sociopolitical domains to the logic of capital (Gray, Dean, Agilias, Howard, and Schubert, 2015; Hay and Kapitzke, 2009). The neoliberal involves "the elevation of calculative logics of economic relations over political ones" (Clarke, 2010, 385). At the same time, neoliberalism introduces a mode of thinking, or a discursive framework, that encourages the construction of a self that is autonomous, individualistic, and competitive. Furthermore, a central premise of neoliberal governance is the expectation that people are self-governing individuals who are enterprising, self-sufficient, and self-directing (Clarke, 2010; Hay and Kapitzke, 2009; Rose, 1999). Neoliberalism, through the introduction of a market orientation in the public social sphere, supports profit making and a corporate approach to education in the public university (Moffatt et al., 2016; Turk, 2008a, 2008b).

Neoliberalism, while focused on the promotion of individual responsibility, liberty, and freedom, is in fact one of those discursive structures that supports capitalism as if it were a stable social structure. There is a contradictory nature to neoliberalism, since through this discourse there is an active re-creation of markets as an "exercise of freedom" alongside an intensified regulation of the roles and responsibilities of those who are governed (Gray et al., 2015). In this manner, neoliberalism creates, disseminates, and modifies discourses that both help capital to adapt to crises of capitalism and maintain capitalist power in the political sphere (Hay and Kapitzke, 2009).

Neoliberalism is more than an economic model or broad structural concern. From a Foucauldian perspective, it is an active approach to the management of people that includes a

26

combination of pervasive and not always transparent regimes of discipline, regulation, governance, and biopolitics. According to Foucault, neoliberalism is not a broad structure of economic relationships or ideology so much as a practical approach to governing (Gray et al., 2015). It is a set of practices in political sovereignty with a method and technique for governance (Gray et al., 2015). Through this network of practices, order is guaranteed. Neoliberalism as "an art of government means focusing on the local, contingent conditions of its emergence, the specific rationalities it employs, and, in particular, the kinds of technologies through which it operates. It means approaching neoliberalism not just as a political philosophy or an ideology but also as a way of thinking about problems and rendering them actionable" (Gray et al. 2015, 382).

The neoliberal penetrates deeply within the university setting, so much so that teaching practices, social relationships, and personal subjectivity within the classroom are defined by neoliberal precepts (Macias, 2015; Moffatt et al., 2016; Moffatt et al., 2018). In other words, neoliberalism can be understood both as a material and linguistic practice that entails a series of discursive practices that define institutions and as the subjectivity of people within those institutions (Macias, 2015). The study of neoliberalism requires the study of policy statements and legislative requirements. Just as importantly, it requires a reflection on our ways of thinking and our practices with the educational system and the classroom.

New Managerialism

Based on the neoliberal concept that each of us is a self-defined economic individual, new managerialism has become the principle form of neoliberal governance in the Western postsecondary educational sector and, increasingly, in the social service sector (Anderson, 2006; Brehony and Deem, 2005; Deem, 2008; Preston and Aslett, 2014). New managerialism, rooted in the general shift to neoliberalism throughout North America and Europe since the 1980s, is a governing discourse that facilitates the institutional shifts within postsecondary education toward a corporate model of governance (Anderson, 2006; Deem et al., 2007).

New managerialism has been key in the shifts in postsecondary education, including its increased focus on competition, managerialism, and regulatory accountability. New managerialism is also tied to the commercial production of research outcomes that enhance national competitiveness. The internationalization of new managerialism has been enacted through bodies such as the World Trade Organization and the European Union (King, 2010; Moffatt et al., 2018).

A central feature of new managerialism is the focus on efficiency, or doing more with less. In the name of efficiency and accountability, new managerialism emphasizes control over the individual performance of both students and educators. The calculative logic of the aforementioned economic principles that define neoliberalism becomes a principle form of governance of students and professors. Educators and students are measured through continuous performance measurements, as well as the auditing of labor practices (Anderson, 2006; Brehony and Deem, 2005; Bruneau and Savage, 2002; Deem, 2008). In these ways,

28

teaching and research become subsumed within the logic of management (Deem, 2008).

New managerialism changes the culture of universities from one guided by collegial norms to one characterized by managerial and corporate-oriented ways of operation (Preston and Aslett, 2014; Woodhouse, 2009). The increase in measures of accountability and the performance assessment of individuals mentioned earlier undermine existing collegial governance structures in the university. These measures also lead to more bureaucratic control and oversight (Anderson, 2006; Fanghanel and Trowler, 2008). The contemporary politics of new managerialism is focused on economy, efficiency, and effectiveness in the delivery of higher education. These three concepts assume a stable social order within which people and institutions can make adjustments that are measured through empirical facts, such as performance indicators and outcome measures (Anderson, 2006; Fanghanel and Trowler, 2008; Moffatt, 2012c).

The pressures for change in the university setting lead to the promotion of the roles of managers and entrepreneurs, so much so that those subjectivities are most valued in the neoliberal regime expressed through new managerialism (Moffatt et al., 2016; Todd et al., 2017). These pressures for change call into question the existing practices of institutional actors, such as those of the educator and the student (Moffatt et al., 2016; Todd et al., 2017). Through the attempt to control them and to measure their practice through new managerialism, actors are pressured within universities to be ready at all times to accept organizational change (Pietroni, 1995; Woodhouse, 2009). The manager becomes important as a person who will guide the university through the necessary process of resourcing efficiencies. In the university sector, this logic is tied not only to administration of the institution but also to the training of students as entrepreneurs and managers (Moffatt et al., 2016; Peters and Besley, 2008). A greater emphasis on constant demands for evaluation contributes to organizational change that weakens postsecondary institutions' historical purpose, which was based on liberal values and critical thinking (Anderson, 2006; Ball, 2012; Davies, 2005; Ginsberg, 2011).

The discursive practices associated with neoliberalism and new managerialism are part of the context of precariousness and instability that characterizes our social and economic systems. Rather than originating from an intention to stabilize the social order, the discourses of neoliberalism and new managerialism are meant to induce constant change within postsecondary education. A reflective approach to practice and knowledge construction allows educators to face directly a destabilized social order through critical inquiry (Pietroni, 1995), in spite of the lack of stability that is obscured by neoliberal and new managerial discourses.

Technological Worldview

The technological worldview in the field of social work education is consistent with Foucault's analysis of Enlightenment thought and modernity. Modernity, according to Foucault (1973), was a coherent project characterized by the drive to explain social conditions through taxonomy. Universal reason was a central epistemological construction of modernity. Modern social change then occurred through the collection of scientific facts that helped us to better understand the stable social order.

Practices derived from scientific study were enacted through state institutions (Hansen, 1997; Irving, 1999; Moffatt, 2001a).

In my archival research on knowledge claims in social work, I have noted a structure of thought or discursive regime based in technique or the technological worldview. Technological discourse in social work is defined by the parameters of technical rationality, the appeal to expertise, the value of efficiency, reductionist thinking, individualism, and confidence in progress. This discursive regime existed in North American social work education during the rise of the professions in the interwar years of the 1920s and 1930s. The technological point of view both constrained and defined the parameters of people's understanding of social relations. It was highly valued by some social work educators and therefore was promoted as the responsible means of professionalization. Some social work academics felt that this approach to the profession and social change would assist with the maintenance of social order during the interwar years (Moffatt, 2001a). The discourse of technology in the field of social work is an attempt to create a definitive way of knowing (Moffatt, 2001a).

At the same time, the technological point of view was highly contested, since some social workers found dangers in technology and the science of social relations. To those people, the technological point of view simplified complex human relations and did not effectively deal with more elusive ways of thinking about social problems and how to address the social good. Social work academics who challenged technology drew on a mixture of approaches, including social activism, poetry, idealism, sociology, political science, and philosophy (Moffatt, 2001a).

The technological worldview and neoliberal approaches to education are active within our contemporary discursive regime.

31

With the rise of the knowledge economy, promoted by the Organisation for Economic Co-operation and Development, education became focused on knowledge-intensive productivity and the globalization of economics (Bullen, Faheny, and Kenway, 2006). Furthermore, in the knowledge economy, universities are perceived to be critical to economic competitiveness, so higher education policy models based on economic competition are particularly influential (Fanghanel and Trowler, 2008; King, 2010). At the same time, the purpose of the university, as defined by the knowledge economy, has shifted to focus more clearly on the resource and labor needs of the private corporate sector (Turk, 2000, 2008a, 2008b; Woodhouse, 2009). One of the norms associated with the knowledge economy is the ability of a nation-state to be supple in social relations in order to restructure in support of knowledge creation as an economic resource (Bullen et al., 2006; Wersun, 2010). Like the discursive frames of neoliberalism and new managerialism, the technological frame alludes to stability while in fact promoting flexibility and the constant restructuring of interpersonal and social relations (Franklin, 1999).

The frameworks that have been presented here—neoliberalism, new managerialism, and the technological worldview—create pressures on the power relations and social dynamics of the classroom. Through the expectations and social roles articulated by the three overlapping discursive regimes, both the student and the professor are socially constituted so that they need to be ready to be supple agents who can adjust to economic, global change. In this context, the social roles of consumer, manager, entrepreneur, and innovator become highly valued and the discourse of the university is reconstructed to make these identities present (Moffatt et al., 2016; Todd et al., 2017). This is part of the tangle of economic, juridical, and governing concepts that construct our classroom reality.

In spite of our best attempts to protect our classrooms from broader troubling cultural politics and social relations, these discursive and epistemic pressures are present in the classroom. They are introduced through the measures of student and professor worth, through the objectives and goals of the university, through media infiltration of the classroom, and, most significantly, through the subjective expectations of both the student and the professor (Preston and Aslett, 2014; Yee and Wagner, 2013).

The discursive frameworks I have described create pressure to teach about a particular type of professional social worker. The overall climate of the professional classroom is focused on enhancing individualism and competition among professionals. The professional social worker is increasingly under pressure to create knowledge through the discourse of technology that values reductive measures and efficient measurement in order to track the most marginalized populations. The social work professional, defined by neoliberal discourse, is skilled at technical applications to professional practice, is distant in her or his relationships with service users, and is individualistic in her or his approach to social problems (Franklin, 1999). The practice of the professional in a contemporary context is focused on concrete products for consumption.

I believe the structuring of thought and practice outlined here operates as the type of episteme described earlier. The episteme focused on certitude works to obscure the precarious nature of our social and economic relationships, as well as to counter a fear of those precarious relationships. In addition, a principal purpose of the contemporary episteme is to spread technological certitude as an economic driver through reductive and determinate measures of social relationships. This episteme needs to be open to critical reflection since it acts as a normative structure both for how we feel and for how we make ourselves present (Grant, 1959; Irving, 1999).

The frameworks of neoliberalism, new managerialism, and technology are meant to create a sense of certitude through the knowledge claims linked to power. These taken-for-granted discursive structures promote autonomy and individualism, as well as making people personally responsible for their disadvantages rather than understanding them as an effect of social, economic relations. It is difficult to teach reflection in the context of such powerful discursive regimes, since reflection itself can become a measurable technique or replicable practice. If not carefully considered, in the context of new managerialism, reflection becomes little more than a technique whereby reflective practice becomes one of the standardized and reductive measures of personal self-worth and professional efficacy. These replicable techniques, in turn, can become a form of governance and control not only of others but also of the personal, professional self.

To avoid casting reflection as a measurable outcome and a product of professional service, we can engage in a history of the present by documenting our technique-driven curricula and practices, as well as recognizing systems of governance that make it difficult to hear the actors, including student and educator, within the postsecondary educational system. Also, reflection can help us understand shifting relations and confused identities in the context of constant neoliberal change and the shifting tangle of expectations arising from managerialism, neoliberalism, and technology.

How do we get outside the episteme of certainty? How do we reflect on broad epistemic influences in the classroom? How, in a time of competition, individualization, and reductive measurement, do we acknowledge networks of relations that can be both dangerous and productive? A means of addressing the taken-for-granted quality of these frameworks is for the educator to engage, alongside the students, in a form of reflection leading to critical analysis. I contend that we should teach directly to the issues associated with and processes unleashed by precariousness in order to face more clearly the social, economic, and cultural forces of capitalism. We can help students to reflect on our own and their precariousness while being sensitive to the precariousness of social work service users.

PRECARIOUS LIFE

The Profession of Social Work: Attempts at Stability in Change

Between World War I and World War II, the secular profession of social work was created in North America. Before this, much social service delivery was associated with faith-based voluntary services. Service providers, or *friendly visitors*, most often sponsored by churches, decided who was worthy and unworthy of support. The creation of a professional body of social workers was thought by many to be a progressive move from the intermittent visits and subjective judgments of these friendly visitors (Moffatt, 2001a; Shore, 1987; Valverde, 1991). Underlying the rise of social work was an assumption that social workers were to become long-term professional employees in permanent institutions.

35

Those institutions were most often imagined as state bureaucracies based on governing principles of community care and social protection (Moffatt, 2001a; Shore, 1987).

Neutrality of judgment was a value for some who pushed for a professional approach tied to a bureaucratic structure of public service. For many, it was a stride forward to imagine a world where people were served by professionals who were committed to social protection and based their judgments of need on objective and neutral measures. A debate ensued during the founding years of secular social work about the foundational knowledge required. The philosophy of a full-time profession of social work to be delivered through state programs and nonprofit voluntary agencies was also highly contested. The disagreement among social work academics and practitioners led to a discussion about whether social work engagement should be political and systematic, philosophical and value driven, based in community caring and philanthropy, or technologically driven, scientific, and objective (Moffatt, 2001a).

All these historical paradigms were based on the optimistic assumption of a stable and enduring profession of social work. Social workers became preoccupied with rigor, respectability, accountability, and service. These qualities of knowledge and practice would ensure the employability of the workers and correct for past workers' errors arising from arbitrary and subjective judgments informed by religious precepts and values not always shared by the service users. The new profession of social work during the interwar years would be guided by the triad of a universal code of ethics, state-supported institutions, and a national body of like-minded and disciplined professionals. This optimistic notion of social work imagined a progressive future characterized by an advanced and more stable social order (Moffatt, 2001a).

The Context of Liquid Modernity

In contrast to this historical vision of social work based on principles of stability and social care, we currently are living through
a time in which social and economic structures are built on
principles of uncertainty and precariousness (Bauman, 2005,
2011, 2012; Moffatt et al., 2009). The responsibility for solving
social quandaries in this context has shifted from the collective
to the individual (Bauman, 2005, 2012). Neoliberal notions of
the individual as enterprising, self-directing, and self-sufficient
reinforce this shift of responsibility and play into this seismic
change in attitude and social beliefs (Gray et al., 2015).

Bauman (2005, 2012) refers to this time when social structure is based on fluid relationships with social structures in constant flux as the era of *liquid modernity*. He (2005, 2012) explains
that the modern context of education has been shifting from the
"solid" to the "liquid" phase. In an era of liquid modernity, "all
social forms melt faster than the new ones can be cast" (Bauman, 2005, 303). Since those social structures that allow for
longer-term planning are in retreat, we are in a constant state of
flux. Furthermore, Bauman (2012) cautions that the impact of
economic and social uncertainty is unevenly distributed according to one's gender, race, and nationality. The tenuousness of
social relations is heightened by changes in our social structure,
so much so that the foundation and possibility of human solidarity are challenged (Bauman, 2005, 2012; George, Moffatt,
Alphonse, et al., 2009).

The frail, impermanent nature of social relations that results
from the discourses of global capitalism is exacerbated by the lack
of political commitment to social protection or communal insurance. Historically, a number of functions tied to the state, such

as education, social welfare programs, health services, and social insurance, were in place to help make the individual more secure and the social structure more stable (Bauman, 2005; Moffatt, 2001a). Social forms that helped to construct security and long-term planning, such as the life-long employment described earlier for those in the profession of social work, no longer serve as a frame of reference for planning the future. The shift away from public responsibility, manifested in decreased funding to educational and social welfare pursuits, contributes to the tenuous nature of social relations (Aronson and Sammon, 2000; Sewpaul, 2006).

In addition, educational and welfare functions are increasingly being defined in an international context without reference to the local (Bauman, 2011; George, Moffatt, Alphonse, et al., 2009; Moffatt et al., 2016). The social domains of welfare are being transferred to the private sector or defined by a private-sector ethos. Decision-making power circulates among international corporate and voluntary organizations at the same time that nation-states are shedding their welfare functions. In this manner, those people in the private sector who influence well-being at the local level become ungovernable because of their ability to communicate across borders and shift resources according to the profit motive (Bauman, 2005, 2011).

As a result of this sense of instability, people see the future as a source of anxiety because of its unpredictability. In this global social context, the individual is preoccupied with survival and "staving off the fall" (Bauman, 2005, 307). The individual's progress is not so much about improving one's lot but rather about avoiding being left behind, as well as avoiding being excluded from social and economic spheres that support social and economic well-being (Bauman, 2005; Moffatt et al., 2018).

While concerns about accountability, service, rigor, and respectability continue to be central to the profession, the new discourses of stability, such as evidence, management, and competition, that drive new managerial and neoliberal discursive frames are infiltrating the fields of social work and education to provide a new logic for the stable growth of the profession (Gray et al., 2015; Moffatt et al., 2018). At the same time, the aforementioned discourses include language that suggests that permanence is no longer imaginable for the profession. For example, the language of social innovation tied to productivity suggests that possibilities for social work education and practice are connected to change rather than stability (Moffatt et al., 2016).

In the time of liquid modernity, we lurch through life with a series of abrupt endings and new beginnings. The life of the individual is best understood as a life of episodes rather than a long life leading to long-term security. Now it is difficult for worker, client, student, or educator to define a "life project" (Bauman, 2005). In this shifting social context, the concept of an education that equips students for an unchanging world and a stable social order is no longer applicable. Also, the goal of preparing students through education for full employment in an ethics-based, stable profession becomes less possible. There are not social work practices that prepare one for a permanent career based on a life-long project. Social work practices need to be thought of in the context of continuous change, in which organizational structures, language, and categories of thinking and practice are being erased (Pietroni, 1995). The whole educational enterprise is no longer a starting point that provides foundational knowledge for a lifelong career in an unchanging profession.

Precariousness

In addition to the increasing level of precariousness that is tied to rapid changes in social structures, there exists a heightened sociocultural aversion to discussing precariousness as a social concept (see Butler, 2006a). The discussions of precariousness, vulnerability, and marginalization that are so central to the social work profession (Witkin, 2012b, 2014a) are more difficult to sustain politically (Butler, 2006a). These discussions bring up anxiety not only about the marginalized people social work students wish to serve but also about the social and economic possibilities for the students and instructors themselves. This inability to discuss our precarious existence silences discussion of the vulnerability of all people (Moffatt et al., 2018).

According to Butler (2006b), with the advent of the war against terrorism, the open discussion of this form of precariousness and vulnerability was foreclosed. Since September 11, 2001, when terrorists flew planes into the Twin Towers of the World Trade Center—the emblems of both global capitalism and American nationalism—Americans have been unable to discuss the shared nature of precariousness. Furthermore, the manipulation and control of media have put a stranglehold on our ability to understand the precariousness of contemporary life.

To discuss the most vulnerable people among us makes transparent our shared responsibility to address precariousness and vulnerability. According to Butler (2006c), the dire consequence of avoiding this discussion is that vulnerable people disappear, since there are no utterances about them. In other words, those people who are most vulnerable are not part of our discourse because they force us to face the shared precariousness and social vulnerability that is a characteristic of contemporary human existence (Butler, 2006b, 2006c).

If we engage in a politics that includes a discussion of precariousness, we begin to ask who has disappeared from the public record and what purpose their disappearance serves. By addressing precariousness, we make sure that those who have disappeared become visible and that if they have no voice, others will make noise on their behalf (Butler, 2006b). This counterpolitic involves disrupting the public sphere to speak to the knowledge that is needed to understand the value of human life. Such value is brought to the fore when we discuss "who has been lost" and what violence has been wrought on the most precarious people (Butler, 2006b).

For social workers who deal with marginalized and vulnerable people in their daily practice, keeping alive the discussion of shared vulnerability is an ethical imperative. Professionals involved in caring for disadvantaged populations are keenly aware of the shared precariousness of human existence, as well as the unequal social distribution of risk (see Witkin, 2012b, 2014a). The ethical imperative of acknowledging shared vulnerability and of being a witness to precariousness is especially relevant in light of the increased vulnerability and precariousness discussed by Bauman. The exercise of making visible those people who might disappear without utterance is particularly important, since I teach in classrooms where students have also experienced marginalization arising from gender, race, ability, and sexuality in their daily lives while trying to work with communities of people who have been marginalized by the very neoliberal forces that are shaping the governance of the university.

POSTMODERN SOCIAL WORK

The pedagogical question for me is how to help students under-stand constraining discourses of thought, such as neoliberalism, new managerialism, and technological thought, within the context of the precariousness of human existence. Postmodern theory is well suited to the kind of pedagogical concerns I seek to address. Postmodern social workers are concerned with the social construction of disadvantage, as well as how thought and discourse create inclusions and exclusions (Healy, 2005; Ungar, 2004). At the same time, a postmodern approach allows one to move through rapid social change by "moving away from reduc-tionist philosophies and towards more holistic or integrative ways of thinking in which clusters of ideas and practices can move in varying ways through more transitional forms of organisation. In this new world flexible and short life structures are both nec-essary and desirable" (Pietroni, 1995, 34). Social workers draw-ing on a postmodern framework have a similar approach to the social-constructionist approaches to social work outlined in chapter 3. Both approaches see social work concepts and prac-tices as socially constructed (Healy, 2005; Parton, 2009; Witkin, 2017).

Irving argues that the "central thrust of modernity has been to invent order, promote certainty and, most important, to link technology and progress" (1994, 22). Postmodern social work theory and practice have split from modernist thinking, which is characterized by a desire to find answers to questions with cer-titude and a tendency to assume that such certitude in thought leads to a better future (Irving, 1994, 1999; Parton, 2009; Wit-kin, 2017). Postmodern approaches to social work also break from Enlightenment thinking, which seeks to find definitive and central truths about the social world (Irving, 1994; Parton, 2009). Key concepts of the Enlightenment, such as the narrow definition of reason and the elevation of reason to a preferred way of knowing, as well as the solution to most problems (Irving, 1994; Healy, 2005; Parton, 2009; Pon et al., 2011; Witkin, 2017), are anathema to postmodernists. Similarly, post-modernists avoid universally applying social concepts to people's existence or proposing overarching explanations of the social world (Parton, 2009; Pon, 2009; Tejaswini and Ennis, 2018; Witkin, 2017). Such overarching concepts are often referred to as metanarratives, and they assume the application of thought will lead to progress and can be applied universally across diverse groups (Irving, 1994; Parton, 2009). In fact, the very notion of progress is brought into question with a postmodern perspective (Irving, 1994).

The literature of postmodern social work has drawn extensively on Foucauldian definitions of power (Chambon, Irving, and Epstein, 1999; Fook, 2002; Irving, 1999; Tejaswini and Ennis, 2018). Foucault's concept of power, which is referred to throughout this book, includes the following precepts:

- Power is exercised, not possessed.
- Power and knowledge are linked.
- Power is present at all times.
- Power is productive rather than repressive.
- Expressions of power differ widely according to setting, interactions, and subjectivities. (Chambon et al., 1999; Fook, 2002; Healy, 2005)

Foucault invites us to think through how power is exercised in particular locations, such as the classroom, and institutions, including the university (Fook and Gardner, 2007; N. Gould and Baldwin, 2004; Healy, 2005). Taken-for-granted practices of social work such as helping, empowering, and emancipation are brought into question for the way they contribute to networks of power and assumptions about both the helper and the service user (Chambon, 1999; Healy, 2005; Heron, 2005; Pease, 2002; Pon et al., 2011). Postmodern thinkers draw on concepts of power to reflect critically on the way that our practices contribute to the surveillance and discipline of each other, as well as the service user (Healy, 2005; Moffatt, 1999a).

The postmodern approach also is based on a critical analysis of discourse. A key element of postmodern thinking, according to Witkin, is that "language is viewed as a constitutive force and objects in the world are discursively produced" (2014a, 14). According to Healy (2005, 199), *discourse* refers to the language practices through which knowledge, truth, our sense of self, and social relations are constructed. Particular attention is given by postmodern social work theorists to opening up alternative discourses for understanding the needs of service users by moving away from the scientific discourses that favor interpretation based on pathology and reductive measures of worth. Postmodern thinkers encourage us to move from individualistic and essentialist approaches to understanding the social and interpersonal nature of humans and their needs (Chambon et al., 1999; Healy, 2005; Parton, 2009; Pon, 2009). The conceptual lens of postmodern social work helps us to understand how the strategic interlinking of knowledge and power has privileged and prioritized professional knowledge over other types of knowledge (Fook, 2002; Heron, 2005; Witkin, 2017).

In addition, postmodernists acknowledge that there are multiple discourses within the field of social work and that these discourses are in tension with each other at times. They are concerned with how discourses in the field of social service construct our ways of knowing, as well as how we think about and construct service users' identities (Chambon, 1994; Healy, 2005; Irving, 2014). Since discourses are not fixed and rigid, they combine and operate in many ways in our educational and social service institutions to influence both social work practice and thought (Chambon, 1994; Fook, 2002; Healy, 2005; Witkin, 2014a).

Language plays a key role in the formation of the self, thought, and subjectivity (Howe cited in Parton, 2009). Postmodernists assert that language and discourse create the possibility of an identity and that an array of factors, such as culture, language, a historical understanding of social concepts, interpersonal relations, and space, all lead to the expression of a wide range of identities, all of which are socially constructed (Irving, 1994, 2014; Irving and Moffatt, 2002). In fact, since there is a distrust of concepts such as an enduring identity that is fixed over time, the terms *subjectivity* and *self* are more congruent with postmodern thought than the concept of identity is. Rather than be concerned solely about identity, we think through our self and how it is formed in differing contexts (Fook, 2014; Healy, 2005).

All this leads to a practice of social work that is open to ambivalence, change, fragmentation, and discontinuity not only in practice but also in how social workers think about the social fabric (Fook, 2011; Healy, 2005; Irving, 1994; Irving and Young, 2002; Pease and Fook, 1999; Todd, 2012). Rather than seek definitive responses, universally applicable practices, and progressive developmental thinking to understand social structures and social relations, postmodernists are open to rupture, eccentricity, and the limits of understanding or *not knowing* (Healy,

2005; Irving, 1994; Kumsa, 2006; Moffatt, 2001a; Phillips, 2007; Todd, 2007). The postmodern framework for teaching invites us to reconsider taken-for-granted approaches to thinking (Irving and Young, 2002; Witkin, 2017), such as conceptualizing social structures as stable and permanent, as well as the ability to measure reality in precise ways (Moffatt, 2017; Witkin, 2017). It intentionally avoids closed and "perfect" forms of social concepts (Chambon et al., 1999; Irving, 1999; Irving and Moffatt, 2002).

A central postmodern practice is the deconstruction and reconstruction of discourses, knowledge, and social relationships (Fook, 2016; Healy, 2005; Morley, 2014; Pease, 2002; Todd, 2007). Deconstruction allows the educator to break apart and question categorical thinking and reimagine relationships by doing the following:

- Deconstructing the creation of dualisms in thought (Fook, 2016; Healy, 2005; Hickson, 2016)
- Questioning the taken-for-granted or implied assumptions of our thought and language (Fook and Gardner, 2007; Irving, 1994; Todd, 2007)
- Analyzing power (Fook and Gardner, 2007; Hickson, 2016; Pease, 2002; Tejaswini and Ennis, 2018; Witkin, 2017)
- Imagining new possibilities (Fook and Gardner, 2007; Healy, 2000, 2005; Irving, 1994, 2014; Morley, 2014; Pease, 2002; Pease and Fook, 1999)

In fact, one should not seek the truth that lies below the surface of relationships and language but instead acknowledge that multiple truths exist because of the wide range of contexts, languages, images, subcultures, and cultures (Chambon, 1999;

Fook and Gardner, 2007; Hickson, 2016; Irving, 1994, 2014; Moffatt, 2012a, 2012e; Parton, 2009; Todd, 2007; Witkin, 2017). In particular, postmodern thought works against simple binaries, such as oppressed/oppressor, male/female, normal/abnormal, and researcher/researched (Fook and Napier, 2000; Healy, 2005; Irving, 2014, Kumsa, 2006; Morley, 2014; Pon et al., 2011).

This deconstruction of knowledge, power, relationships, and practice allows the student or social worker to engage in an exercise of reconstruction. Through a series of questions and actions, a practitioner can think through and act on a new meaning for a practice situation (Fook, 2002; Fook and Gardner, 2007; Morley, 2014). The reconstruction allows for the possibility of new discourses, languages, practices, and processes (Fook, 2016; Todd, 2005, 2007). It also allows for students and practitioners to feel differently about their work by becoming active agents as they uncover "options that may have been rendered invisible by dominant discourses" or metanarratives (Morley, 2014, 1429).

Postmodern thought offers a conceptual frame for teaching that addresses the increased precariousness of our social and economic spheres. This frame considers both the discursive regime within which we conceptualize thought and practice (neoliberalism, new managerialism, a technological worldview) and the limits of classroom discourse (competition, individualism, technique-driven interaction). Most importantly, the postmodern seeks to "impart a stronger sense of the un-presentable" (Nicholls, 1991, 4). In a time of precariousness and uncertainty, we seek to understand what "constructs knowledge in practice, particularly what counts as true and sayable and what is considered false or unsayable" (Healy, 2005, 199). It is my hope to help students to speak for and about those who have become invisible in the discussion. It is this in "intolerable present" that I wish to interrogate the importance of "making a mark" for others (Butler, 2006b).

I am interested in correcting for the absences in our classroom, which may include the following:

- Recognizing the voices of those who have been excluded (Foucault, 1979; Moffatt, 2001b)
- Uncovering the limits of the discourses of neoliberalism, new managerialism, and technology (Foucault, 1979; Moffatt et al., 2016)
- Discussing the anxiety associated with precariousness (Bauman, 2012; Moffatt et al., 2018)
- Helping us find the voices of those who have been lost (Butler, 2006b, 2006c)

I am attentive as an educator to those people who are not heard from in the classroom, as well as those who are slipping away from our shared social consciousness.

A central objective of teaching that is sensitive to constant social change and precariousness is to respect a wide variety of utterances within the classroom in order to give voice to those people and communities that have been "left behind." The students then become involved in creating a mode of knowledge particular to their subjective experience. Through this imagination of thought, students can become knowledge creators and agents with voice (Pease, 2002; Witkin, 2012a, 2014a). At times, we can fit differing images and sources together loosely to create the conditions of imagination and wonderment and to allow for the possibility of reflection (Irving and Moffatt, 2002; Irving and Young, 2002; Wehbi, El-Lahib, Perreault-Laird, and Zakharova, 2018).

In this manner, an educator can help students become active agents by understanding the logic of dominant discourses, as well as by dismantling those discourses. I hope to help students imagine thought as politicized, subjective, open, and dynamic (Jorgensen and Yob, 2013). Social processes can be revealed through policy analysis, media studies, gender studies, and cultural studies. The precarious nature of social existence can be shown through images, video clips, personal narratives, and theory.

With this approach to education, our interpersonal relationships in the classroom are influenced by the broadest social structures and myths of knowing, but these structures and myths are not the sole determinant of relationships. Thus, although broad conceptualizations of social, political, and economic conditions can be a useful frame for understanding troubling social relationships and marginalization, I avoid focusing on social and economic context as an abstraction that is separate from personal practice (Moffatt, 2001b; Moffatt et al., 2005). The idea is to help students understand the interplay of both the general and the specific (Moffatt et al., 2005). The traditional split in social thought between the macro and the micro fades away (Chambon, 1999; Moffatt, 1999a, 1999b, 2001b; Sinding and Barnes, 2015).

REFLECTION: TEACHING TO PRECARIOUSNESS

In a required course for a master's degree focused on marginalization, I present ideas of risk, uncertainty, and precariousness.

I also describe the discursive structures that constrain our thought. I then ask students to discuss a crisis of our time that contributes to a sense of precariousness. In the fall of 2014, those risks were manifested in the ISIS insurgency and an attack on a military person in Canada's national capital. In the fall of 2015, precariousness was manifested in massive displacements of people, such as in the Syrian refugee crisis in Europe. At other times, the precariousness named by students had to do with economic instability (the economic crisis of 2008), warfare (the Iraq War), and disease, including the ongoing pandemic of AIDS, as well as Ebola and SARS. More recently, precariousness has been tied to the breakdown of political consensus about internationalization, with a rise in the influence of right-wing, nationalist, and exclusionary groups. Students have commented on all these phenomena as events that have destabilized their sense of self and sense of confidence in our social systems.

One such topic was the spread of Ebola in Africa and the perceived risk of contagion internationally. In one of my courses, we reflected on both emotional reactions to and cognitive understandings of the disease. Specifically, students discussed the feeling of being unmoored or at risk in general. The response in the classroom was wide ranging, from expressions of fear to a calm, critical analysis of media's misrepresentation of the disease. For some students who worked in large, urban, cosmopolitan health settings, the fear was palpable. In one case, a student who worked in a health setting noted that preparations for the possibility of pandemic were already in place at her job. In another case, the student attended a health clinic as a client but was conscious of health-care personnel suiting up to prevent contact with a potentially contaminated person. Another student who works in public health worried about the spread of the disease at her workplace. These institutional practices in the students' daily lives evoked fear.

Other students worried that the response of fear was tied to the racist treatment of African people. A long discussion ensued about the representation of the African continent in media. Racist imagery ranged from depictions of Africans as "primitive" people who did not understand the superiority of Western medicine to images of foreign health-care workers in full-body protective suits while black people were exposed without protection. Perhaps the most shocking was the image in the *New York Times* of a young child lying in front of a clinic, which featured a caption about the inferior condition of African health care. This photo can be interpreted in a number of ways, including as evidence that the African health-care system fails in comparison with the privatized American health system. There seemed to be a consensus among students that media representation made a troubling suggestion that Africans had failed to deal with unhealthy people in distress.

Perhaps more compelling were the students who used their personal experience to state facts about the disease—the students who risked an utterance. A student born in the Philippines stated, "We have Ebola in the Philippines and we have a protective measure. We have had it for years. It can be isolated from island to island." Also, a student from Eritrea said that in Eritrean culture, it is believed that people should not die alone, so people break into the quarantine camps that were set up to slow spread of the disease to be with loved ones as they die; they know that it is a death sentence to be sent to quarantine.

In a classroom discussion staged in this manner, a multiplicity of viewpoints can be imagined and each student can engage according to his or her distinct subjectivity. The point of this

51

exercise is not to confirm the factual evidence of each truth claim among the participants in the classroom. Rather, it offers the opportunity for an important discussion about the construction of the present and the social and health responses to the disease. It allows students to map the strategies of power and knowledge. An open discussion also allows each subjective knowledge claim in the classroom to have merit. At times, the subjectivity of students disrupts the taken-for-granted conceptual understanding of the topic. Speaking from subjective experience creates possibilities for connections, with no one person making a deeper claim on the truth.

In addition, Ebola is a point of reflection. It becomes a symbol of the risk and precariousness of our time. Through discussion of a topic such as the cultural import of Ebola, questions arise about colonialism, prejudice, and marginalization, as well as the significance and reliability of visual and textual representations of health and well-being. In our discussion, we reflect on how knowledge about the disease is created both politically and socially, particularly in the colonial context of North America. We also reflect on the nature of both preventative and ameliorative direct practice. Hopefully, each person in the discussion both offers a subjective interpretation and is put in a reflexive position to imagine the limits of his or her own knowledge.

We also become aware of how all images and knowledge claims have the political purpose of protecting us from awareness of the limits of the global economy (Bauman, 2005) or the precariousness of life in North America (Butler, 2006a). In this manner, we deconstruct state-sanctioned knowledge such as new managerialism and neoliberalism while letting eccentric, partial, and specific knowledge of Ebola become present in the classroom.

DISCUSSION

In this chapter, I have made a case for a Foucauldian approach to understanding practices in postsecondary education. Rather than take a binary approach of left-versus-right politics, macro-versus-micro interventions, or progressive-versus-mainstream approaches, I caution that we should be attentive to discursive regimes that both constrain and make possible our modes of practice. I suggest that the interaction of three key constraining discursive structures of contemporary education—neoliberalism, new managerialism, and the technological worldview—create a bias toward measurable, reductive practice; autonomy and individual merit; and capitalist intrusions in our reflective processes. These discursive frameworks strategically attempt to assure us of stability. Yet I argue that the social context of our classroom is one of instability and precariousness. I have identified some of the issues associated with not addressing precariousness. It is my contention that we must teach about and to precariousness in the classroom rather than seek stable structures for understanding social relationships. A postmodern approach to social work can help us think through these pedagogical dilemmas.

Students are constantly reminded that they live in precarious times. Asking them to reflect on such precariousness is not an abstract practice. They are aware of low-paying social service jobs and the precariousness of caring work (Todd et al., 2017). They are aware of the need to work to support their education and that such work is often contract based or project based. They are fully aware of rising housing costs and the lack of affordability in major urban areas. They are aware that in their increasingly large classes, they are not known as individuals.

I hope that by encouraging students to speak about discourse that has been repressed and voices that are not heard, we are engaging in an act of justice in the classroom. I also hope that the new discourses created in the classroom influence the nature of knowledge and the shared experience of knowledge creation. We commence our journey of professional caring not from the point of view of competencies or discursive certainties that neo-liberalism, new managerialism, and technology invite. Rather, we start our caring journey from a point of loss, melancholy, risk, and precariousness.

I believe that this teaching from uncertainty ironically enhances a sense of agency through self-reflection. When the students become aware of the limits of dominant discourse or metanarratives, they are able to express the discourse of those groups that have been silenced and they experience the thrill of hearing the experience and knowledge expressed out loud in public. They also create a new political dynamic in the classroom through disruption of the taken-for-granted.

2

REFLECTIVE SOCIAL WORK PRACTICE

The Social and the Self

Early in my university teaching career, I found the work of Donald Schön a welcome relief from the technique-driven social work practice focused on competencies, outcomes, and efficiencies that are well suited to neoliberal governance. Technique-driven social work also has a close conceptual alliance to new managerialism and the technological worldview. I had worked as a social worker in bureaucratic institutional settings where social work practice was defined more by legislation and policy than by the voices of those who were being served. As a social worker who had worked as a child protection worker in a child welfare agency and later as a community worker within a Canadian federal community development program, I had been engaged in models of technical practice. It became clear to me, during my practice as a child welfare worker, that the mechanisms for measuring the worth of clients and the risk of children ignored social factors, such as the inequitable investigation of racialized families by child welfare workers (Pon, Gosine, and Phillips, 2011). According to Gosine and Pon (2011), racialization is that "social process by which people come to be raced" (136). Those persons are socially constructed to belong to a racial group with certain traits (Dei, 2008; Gosine and Pon, 2011). Racialization occurs when people in positions of dominance combine strategies of power to create discourses about persons according to race; the process of racialization refers to race as a discourse that is created according to social and economic structural needs (Abrams and Moio, 2009). In child welfare settings, for example, racialization occurs alongside other measures of worth of service users (Pon et al., 2011).

In the field of social work, modes of measurement have become increasingly driven by technology as jobs require the completion of online forms. These means of measurement have become more and more abstract from the lived experience of need for families at risk. As a social worker, I had become skilled at employing hidden practices with clients that were not easily tracked within the bureaucratic workplaces such as social service agencies, social assistance offices, and child welfare agencies, so as to avoid the limitations of technical approaches (Moffatt, 1999a, 1999b; K. Smith, 2007).

As I develop my reflective teaching practice and continue my pursuit of questions associated with technologies of practice, I have begun to be aware of the limitations of a singular framework such as Schön's. Although his approach is a worthy open-ended frame for practice that allows for intuition and multiplicity in application, it seems to be constrained as a modernist construct. In this chapter, I outline Schön's thought as a formative framework in the discussion of professional reflective practice. I argue that social work literature enriches the field of reflective practice by focusing not only on the professional but also on the personal self. I argue that a reflective practice that is open to ambivalence and ongoing reflective processes results in a supple understanding of social well-being and social justice.

DONALD SCHÖN

Schön, influenced by John Dewey, was an American philosopher interested in how people "think on their feet." He was a musician as well as theoretician who was actively involved in industry and training. He cofounded the Organization for Social and Technological Innovation and served as director of the Institute for Applied Technology in the National Bureau of Standards at the U.S. Department of Commerce during the Kennedy administration. While at the Massachusetts Institute of Technology, he worked with management theorist Chris Argyris on both individual and organizational learning with a focus on learning systems. Schön's interest in thinking during direct practice led to him to study improvisation and grounded learning (Nelson, 2012).

Schön (1983, 1987) offers a frame to understand unspoken practices and direct involvement with service users. It is a good starting point for a reflective practice of teaching for someone who has been seeking relief from the bureaucratic technologies of social welfare institutions (Moffatt, 1999b). I share Schön's (1983) interest in forms of thinking while engaged in practice. This thinking-in-practice stands in opposition to professional practice, with its technical, rational bent based on rarified models of social structures (Moffatt 1999b; Witkin, 2017). Schön (cited in Bleakley, 1999) challenges the technical approach to practice that is based solely on developmental programs, progressivism, steps or stages, a hierarchy of skills, and an overarching dogma. Such structured interventions, Schön has argued, avoid exposure to the benefits of complexity in direct practice. Also, technical approaches are not true to the chaotic, open-ended, and unpredictable nature of learning (Bleakley, 1999; Schön, 1983, 1987; Moffatt, 1999b, 2001b).

Reflective Artistry Over Technical Rationality

Schön is widely known for his key texts *The Reflective Practitioner* (Schön, 1983), *Educating the Reflective Practitioner* (Schön, 1987), and *Theory in Practice* (Argyris and Schön, 1974/1992). His appeal to those who teach in professional programs is his interest in, and conceptualization of, situated activity and learning. These connect cognitive reaction to direct action, and in his investigation of this intersection, he talks both about professional practice and about the conceptualization of practice. These concepts are useful to professional programs that seek to transcend the traditional boundaries of professional workplaces and educational settings (Dohn, 2011). Schön has wide appeal among theorists who study reflective professional practice. He has been a strong influence in professional postsecondary pedagogy in programs such as nursing (see Cleary, Horsfall, Happell, and Hunt, 2013; Graham, 2017; Hargreaves, 2010; Kinsella, 2007; Nelson, 2012), as well as the health and social care professions (see Askeland and Fook, 2009; Dohn, 2011; Fook and Gardner, 2007; Gould and Baldwin, 2004; Gould and Taylor, 1999; Kinsella, 2010; Moffatt, 1999b; Pietroni, 1995; Willson, 2018).

Schön (1983) intentionally worked to counter a tendency in professional schools to define rigorous professional knowledge through a positivist epistemology of practice. According to Schön (1987), the dominant view of practice in postsecondary educational settings involves the solving of instrumental problems through the application of knowledge and technique. He has argued that this approach is inadequate to understand knowledge in practice (Schön, 1987). In the social context of new managerialism, with the tendency toward empiricism and reductivist measures, Schön's reflective practice offers promise, since it is providing a critique of professional knowledge based solely on technical rationality (Kinsella, 2010).

Schön (1983, 1987) challenges us to rethink dominant or taken-for-granted assumptions about professional knowledge based on technical rationality in order to define a more rigorous practice that includes direct experience. Schön (1987) laments that the dominant paradigm for practice in professional educational settings characterizes "practitioners . . . [as] instrumental problem solvers, who select technical means best suited to particular purposes. Rigorous professional practitioners solve well-formed instrumental problems by applying theory and technique derived from systematic preferably scientific knowledge" (Schön, 1987, 3–4). He argues that this reliance on positivist epistemology excludes those phenomena that are present during lived experience and therefore does not address how we learn through practice. In order to draw on direct practice wisdom, he argues for a dialogue between thought and action so that one becomes more skillful at practice (Schön, 1987).

Practice, according to Schön (1987), needs to be conceptualized so as to include artistry as a practice element that the practitioner brings to divergent scenarios. He was worried that "professionalization meant the replacement of artistry by systematic preferably scientific knowledge" (1987, 14). Rather than seeing practice as the application of instrumental reason, he argues that practice is unstable, uncertain, and unique. If this is the case, then technique cannot be applied uniformly across practice scenarios (Schön, 1987). He writes, "Let us search instead for an epistemology of practice implicit in the artistic, intuitive processes which some practitioners do bring to situations of uncertainty, instability, uniqueness and value conflict" (Schön, 1987, 49).

Tacit Practice and Reflection-in-Action

The artistry of professional practice includes esoteric and powerful versions of competencies that practitioners draw on every day. Such practice artistry includes the elements of recognition, judgment, and skill (Schön, 1987). Schön (cited in Dohn, 2011) begins with the assumption that much of the know-how of practice is both implicit and tacit. Tacit knowledge can involve a discovery during practice that cannot be fully expressed in words. Furthermore, tacit knowledge includes those things we know without fully comprehending how we are able to do so (Argyris and Schön, 1974/1992). By its nature, implicit and tacit knowledge makes it difficult for practitioners to fully articulate their knowledge, since there is no conclusive groundwork to justify the practitioners' actions (Dohn, 2011). In fact, at times, practitioners are not fully aware of the overall pattern of their practice (Argyris and Schön, 1974/1992).

Schön (1992) conceptualized the frames reflection-in-action and reflection-on-action to imagine the integration of reflection with action. Reflection-in-action is central to the artistry of practice since practitioners engage in on-the-spot experiments during their practice (Schön, 1992). Reflection-in-action, likened to jazz improvisation, occurs while one is engaged in practice. By being open to improvisation, the practitioner becomes capable of reflection driven by the unique and indeterminate influences

of direct experience (Bleakley, 1999). Reflection-on-action differs from reflection-in-action since it is a retrospective review of
action. Through the process of reflection-on-action, one thinks
through professional practice carried forward in order to influence future actions (Schön, 1992). Professionals need to be aware
of their strategies in order to set the direction of practice, as well
as to reflect on and change the situation and the values that shape
that practice (Schön, 1983).

Knowledge Creation Through Reflective Practice

These reflective constructs of practice are elaborated further by
the concept knowing-in-action. Since thinking and doing are
interwoven together in a coherent practice, knowing-in-action
is the know-how revealed through intelligent practice. This spon-
taneous and skillful performance of professional practice can
reveal our knowledge even if we cannot clearly articulate this way
of knowing (Schön, 1983). Implicit and tacit knowledge are
interconnected: "Often, we cannot say what it is we know. When
we try to describe it, we find ourselves at a loss or we produce
descriptions that are obviously inappropriate. Our knowing is
ordinarily tacit, implicit in our patterns of action and in our feel
for the stuff with which we are dealing. It seems right to say our
knowing is in our action" (Schön, 1983, 49). Once practitioners
become aware that they construct a reality through their practice, they can also become aware of the variety of tacit frames
available to them (Schön, 1983). Once aware of tacit frames, the
practitioner can develop theories of practice that are theories-
in-use developed through attention to tacit knowledge. Theories-
in-use are structures that contain assumptions about others, the

self, and the environment that act as a microcosm of everyday life (Argyris and Schön, 1974/1992). According to Argyris and Schön (1974/1992), it is important for us to make explicit the theories-in-use or tacit frames we draw on during practice, since it is through these tacit frames that we create the normative structures that guide how we see reality. When these frames are overt, practitioners can question them and test them. In this manner, the practitioner receives additional information from the direct act of practice (Argyris & Schön, 1974/1992). The practitioner becomes aware of alternative ways of framing practice when implicit frames are made explicit. The practitioner can reconsider the norms and values that have been given priority during practice or those that have been left out altogether (Schön, 1983).

REFLECTION: THE LIMITS AND POSSIBILITIES OF SCHÖN'S APPROACH

Part of the appeal of Schön's reflective approach is that it offers vitality to both the worker and the service user, since both are open to growth and change (Schön, 1983, 1987). This openness to change is enhanced through a professional practice that is attentive to changes in direction. Such changes occur both in the direction of practice and in the practice paradigm (Askeland and Fook, 2009; Moffatt, 1999b). Schön's concept of practice allows for paradigm shifts in thought during practice, which is useful in the unstable and precarious social context described in chapter 1.

Schön's reflective practice works against the taken-for-granted assumption that the proper construction of knowledge is technical and rational. He also argues against the assumption that knowledge about practice is best derived from scientific inquiry that is then used in the applied sciences. He is distrustful of practice knowledge as an abstract concept that leads to the proper application of concepts, which in turn leads to the development of technical skills (Nelson, 2012). In other words, Argyris and Schön resist the deductive approach to teaching, which involves creating principles based on empirical observation, then teaching those principles to students (Argyris and Schön, 1974/1992; Nelson, 2012). In this way, Schön resists a purely technical practice defined by a technological point of view. Since he clearly debunks technical rationality as the principal paradigm to understand practice, he addresses through practice some of the biases of both new managerialism and technological discursive frameworks discussed in chapter 1.

Recognition of the ambiguity and indeterminacy of the social world is evident in Schön's call to artistry to navigate uncertainty. Fundamental to his thought about practice as artistry is that both the context of practice and professional practice itself are transient and indeterminate (Kinsella, 2010). He anticipates reflective practice based in postmodernism with his insistence on a radical diversity of situations, social contexts, and interactions. Cognitive structure, values, and action are all up for reconsideration as the reflective practitioner works through a problem or process. Schön's openness to a practice that refuses a duality between thought and action, as well as between knowledge and practice, is well suited to social work thought that considers the changing social, political, and economic environment as central to understanding effective practice.

Furthermore, Schön's thinking is congruent with Michel Foucault's thought, which "overturns two sorts of certainties: an external empirical reality to be perceived and counted, and an internal certainty about a solid subjectivity" (Irving, 1999, 28). Schön is a reflective thinker who argues that values are multiple, shifting, and contextualized. Since he values multiplicity and encourages practitioners to look for the unfamiliar in practice, he opens up the concept of practice as being formed by the unspeakable and the unknowable.

At the same time, Schön might be criticized for viewing the self through a modernist lens. When taking a modernist approach to practice, practitioners assume that the person, whether client or social worker, is biologically and psychologically constitutive. Bleakley (1999) argues that accepting the autonomy of the self is a nonreflexive stance based on modernist assumptions. Irving (1999) further problematizes the unitary concept of the subjective self. The self is never separate from the social forces at play in a situation. Personal autonomy, agency, and the self cannot be perceived as static, since they are not separate from social and cultural relationships (Bleakley, 1999; Irving, 1999, 2014).

Liberal humanism shifts the locus of knowledge and power to the autonomous individual (Gray et al., 2015). Schön remains within this liberal humanist or modernist paradigm. While a strength of his approach is his argument that all practice, including professional practice, is located within the subjective position of the viewer, it seems that his model of reflective practice remains based on humanist principles that assume autonomy as the natural state of the self. A limitation seems to be that even as values and approaches to practice shift, the practitioner's self remains intact.

The autonomy and agency of the individual are forces that are culturally and historically in flux. Both autonomy and agency are discursive effects constructed from the signs, language, and practices that are available to a person (Bleakley, 1999; Scott and Usher, 2011; Trevelyan et al., 2012). It follows that the self and personal agency need to be part of the focus of the reflective interrogation of practice. The educator and student in professional practice settings investigate widely those conditions that make possible the self and the subjective approach to practice. Reflective practice, as argued in chapter 1, must also include reflection about the social possibilities of meaning, as well as those discursive structures that make subjectivity possible (Scott and Usher, 2011).

SOCIAL WORK REFLECTIVE PRACTICE: REFLECTION ON THE SOCIAL AND THE SELF

A social work literature has developed based on similar assumptions of Schön's about working from practice. Social work theorists point to the importance of moving from a dichotomy of theory and practice in order to highlight the value of working from practice experience to generate theory (Béres, 2014; Fook, 1999; Healy, 2000). Reflection allows social workers to put "theories in practice through examining their taken-for-granted assumptions and values in light of their social context" (Gardner, 2012, 105). While Schön includes professional subjective judgment and values within the purview of reflective practice, he stops short of supporting social work's insistence on reflecting on the social context for constructing professional reality and imagining how to change troubling aspects of that context. Social work literature also emphasizes the importance of reflecting on both the personal and the professional self while in practice. The reflective approach to social work practice takes up the challenge of both the social construction of practice and reflecting on the self (Béres, 2014; Fook, 2012; Fook and Kellehear, 2010; Graham, 2017; Irving, 2014; Mandell, 2007, 2008; Miehls and Moffatt, 2000; Moffatt, 2012b, 2012c; Sirotich et al., 2012; Witkin, 2012a, 2014a, 2014b).

According to a Foucauldian understanding of the self, the professional social worker's self is the result of a network of technologies or mechanisms. Chambon (1999) explains that Foucault was interested in the self as the end of inquiry rather than the beginning. There are a variety of modes through which we are made subjects who act in the social world. For example, professionals are constituted through networks of professional practice, institutions (including professional institutions and educational institutions), and the exercise of power and the self (Chambon, 1999). Chambon notes,

By examining practices up close through a magnifying lens (cf Gordon 1986) Foucault brought together into a single fold the two poles of the social work profession that are traditionally kept apart, the micro and macro levels of the person and the environment. He made visible the linkages between individual and society: how institutional practices generate social identities which in turn trigger new knowledge and practices. (1999, 56)

Critical reflection, in this case, involves being aware of, and thinking through, how we are constituted as subjective persons. The reflective process of the professional includes reflection on discourse, such as those discourses outlined in chapter 1, and how those discursive practices are related to networks of power (Chambon, 1999; Trevelyan et al., 2012).

A discussion of the interplay of discourse, knowledge, strategies of power, and the construction of the self can be found in Jan Fook's work. Fook has been influential in the fields of health and social care, as well as pedagogy, through her development of reflective practice. She is known for her international work in critical social work and critical reflection. She is an Australian social worker who has also lived and worked in Canada, the United Sates, and England. She provides training internationally in critical reflection. She is visiting professor at Royal Holloway, University of London, and professor and chair of the Department of Social Work at the University of Vermont.

According to Fook (2012), the reflective practitioner assumes that we share broader social processes and cultures that shape our thinking. These broad relations also influence our approach to practice (Fook, 2012). Rather than apply an abstract concept to proper practice, we become attentive to those processes that construct our practice. This reflective model of critical reflection is influenced by Schön's reflective approach to practice, reflexivity, postmodernism, deconstruction, and critical social theory (Fook and Gardner, 2007). Fook and Gardner (2007) are interested in how knowledge is created in both systematic and informal ways. They argue that knowledge that is drawn on in daily practice is often not fully articulated through concepts.

Since professional practice is constructed socially, Fook argues, "an essential element of critical reflection is that one must be prepared to direct the questioning gaze at oneself" (2012, 220). According to Fook, approaches to reflection in the Western world are too often focused on the need to change others, whether service user, colleague, or student. We solve problems and broader social issues by trying to change the opinions of others. Fundamental change, however, happens when we recognize that we are all part of the problem of, as well as part of the solution to, social ills (Fook, 2012). Reflective practice and research involve looking both inward and outward to understand the links between our social and cultural understandings (Fook and Gardner, 2007).

The self is open to radical reinterpretation and change through this form of critical reflection. The open nature of the reflective process allows us to consider who we are culturally, socially, intellectually, emotionally, and spiritually (Fook and Gardner, 2007; Fook and Kellehear, 2010). Reflective practice engages in all aspects of the self, including the body. The process of reflection is not only about changes in direction and implicit theories of practice; it also incorporates new experiences in our sense of self (Fook and Kellehear, 2010).

Mandell (2008) takes a similar approach to reflective practice by insisting that the change in the self is a central focus of reflective practice. She argues that reflective practitioners need to focus on their own personhood. Her multilayered approach includes consideration of the "more idiosyncratic elements of who we are" (Mandell 2008, 237). Aspects of personhood that are open to reflection include one's personal developmental history, the multiple social identities tied to personal experience, one's socialization, the political milieu within which one operates, and one's education. Reflection involves thinking about who we think we are and how that perception comes about within the context of professional relations of power (Mandell, 2008).

Mandell (2008) is interested in those aspects of the identity of the social work practitioner that operate on the unconscious and the conscious levels in relationships. The focus of reflection needs to be on all aspects of the self, including unconscious thoughts, feelings, or affects that lead to interpersonal eccentricity (Mandell, 2008). According to Mandell (2008), the psychotherapeutic literature on countertransference does not adequately address issues of interpersonal and social power. At the same time, social approaches to reflection, such as the anti-oppression approach, tend to focus on the social identity of the practitioner in the context of social domination arising from race, class, and gender differences. She argues that, too often, this approach, with a focus on privilege, on one hand, and oppression, on the other hand, is too binary. If the self is thought of solely in terms of power relations of dominance and submission, these other aspects of the self are not considered.

Like the authors just discussed, M. Keenan (2012) argues for a social-constructionist perspective in which the gaze is turned on the worker's self in practice. Through reflection on our practice, we are invited to look at the dominant discourses we enact in relationship to the client. The politics of discourse that constructs the client and the power relations between the worker and client inform the possibilities that exist for the client. Keenan argues for replacing either-or choices in practice with both-and constructions, since it is impossible to have a singular answer in therapeutic relationships (Keenan, 2012). She (2012) goes on to argue that nonreflexive practice that does not consider professional discourses and practices risks becoming an oppressive act on its own.

Kumsa takes the integration of reflexive practice and the social construction of the self still further by arguing for "the inseparable inter-wovenness of the personal and the political, the individual and the collective, the ethnic and the national, the local and the global, the past and the future, and the conscious and the unconscious" (2012, 308). She argues that social workers too often take a caring position between the state and the oppressed and this position involves "pointing oppression away from ourselves and abdicating responsibilities" (Kumsa, 2016, 603). She does not reduce the nature of the self to either essence or social construction. The self operates at a level where essence and social construction are interlinked and inseparably interwoven. According to Kumsa, "We become subjects through delicate social processes by which our likes and dislikes are woven into our Self and get lodged in our bodies" (2012, 319).

According to Kumsa (2016), the educator's self is affected by interpersonal contact with students as a result of challenges to basic beliefs and values. As a refugee woman of Oromo descent who was persecuted in Ethiopia, she describes the many shifts in her identity and her political practice. A combination of social experiences, including persecution, flight, resettlement, and racialization, have contributed to her construction as a refugee (Kumsa, 2006). She argues that over time and through differing social experiences tied to social construction and banishment of the other, as well as the social construction of who is normal through the nation-state, she has become socially constructed as a *woman at risk*.

The wealthy, powerful, "democratic" First World order of nations exists only in relation to the weak, poor, and "undemocratic" Third World. Yet the constructed nature of this relationship is obscured in order to hide accountability, responsibility, and privilege in social workers' relationship to the other. How do we take risks in reflecting on the self in order to hold ourselves and our nations accountable for colonial legacies (Kumsa, 2012)? She argues that we do so by reflecting deeply on space, time, the self, and the other and blend these lenses in our analysis and practice (Kumsa, 2006). Critical reflection involves seeing

70

the other inside and the self outside. In other words, the self and other are intertwined in relational processes (Kumsa, 2012). Chambon, Mandell, Fook, Gardner, Keenan, and Kumsa approach reflective practice with a clear focus on how social context shapes our practice and our selves as practitioners and educators. By giving up on the notion of an individualized self, the authors also give up on binary approaches to practice, such as the following:

- Applying theory to practice in a didactic manner
- Separating the social, economic, and cultural realms from the interpersonal and personal realms
- Reinforcing power relations that are defined solely through domination and submission

Since social identity and the discursive construction of the self are part of the focus of reflection, the self is open to change through reflection. These approaches contextualize workers and their sense of self, as well as clients and their sense of self, in social relations and interpersonal professional relationships. Social work approaches to reflective practice also allow the practitioner to reflect on ill-defined influences, such as emotions, the idiosyncratic, and the unconscious.

There is no central core of the social worker self; rather, the self can take on multiple facets (Chambon, 1999; Irving, 1999, Moffatt, 2012a; Sirotich et al., 2012). This radical constructionist sense of self is constructed through the particularities of social context. Because of the multiplicity of social experience and possibilities, a person can create multiple selves (Chambon, 1999; Moffatt, 2012d; Sirotich et al., 2012). Irving (1999, 2014) pushes the radical nature of the self even further. Irving (1999), citing Nietzsche and Foucault, argues that the self is never given, and it does not exist out there for us to discover; rather, it must be created. The self can be wrought with tension and ambivalence, since it represents many possibilities and can be reconfigured (Chambon, 1999; Irving, 1999). In the following section, I argue that social workers' focus on broader social relations, coupled with a focus on the self, leads to a type of supple social justice in social relations. The self is constructed through personal, social, and cultural influences, but it is not constrained by those social influences and is open to significant rethinking and change (Fook and Kellehear, 2010; Irving, 2014).

CRITICAL REFLECTIVE PRACTICE
AS A PROCESS OF JUSTICE

Since social work practice is constructed through economic, cultural, and social influences that become present through discourse, social justice is integral to a critical approach to reflective practice. Critical reflection involves unveiling and thinking about the fundamental bases of our thinking, and it can thus be argued that reflection on broad sociocultural influences becomes an act of social justice (Fook, 2002).

Thinking about fundamental values and cognitive understandings of social relations can lead to an experience of personal and social transformation (Fook, 2012; Fook and Gardner, 2007). Irving (1999) argues for a reflective approach that remains separate from broadly defined social justice principles while not giving up on struggle. He argues, "There is no knowledge that is true in itself, that is independent of the languages and institutions that we create and invent. Empirical reality does not exist as a universal truth but as an unending collection of stories that we tell. Truth is made, not found" (1999, 32). In this conceptualization of truth, there is no social justice that can be defined solely by universal principles, but there are many stories and truths informed by justice (Irving, 1999, 2014). The exercise of defining just behavior from abstract principles creates concepts separate from the troubles of lived experience. These detached concepts can contribute to universalizing experience and impose rigid ways of thinking (Irving, 1999). When we propose a meaning or action, we are proposing one of many possible realities (Witkin 2012a, 2012b).

With this caution in mind, the focus on the self in the context of social relations offers up a supple approach to social justice. Taking the approach to social justice whereby practitioners turn their gaze on themselves makes the practice of social justice changeable and multiple (Fook, 2012). Fook cautions that "it is the people with the strongest commitment to critical and social justice ideals who have the greatest difficulty in either turning the gaze towards themselves, or at least turning it away from other people" (2012, 220). The acts and goals of social justice differ according to the interplay of social and interpersonal dynamics (Fook, 2012). Pyne cautions us to think about "our attachment to our progressive identities, our willingness to claim a higher truth and our tendency to prefer theoretical consistency over genuine curiosity" (2016, 69). Binaries in social justice teaching, such as progressive versus regressive, mainstream versus subversive, or active versus passive, persist in spite of an attempt by many educators to be open to diversity, marginalized identities, and social change. I discuss such binary thinking and its temptations more thoroughly in chapter 4, where I argue, as

REFLECTIVE SOCIAL WORK PRACTICE

Pyne does here, that such thinking can too often position the educator to be disrespectful and, at worst, harmful toward students in the classroom, especially those students, such as trans students, whose identities are nonnormative or absent from classroom discourse (Pyne, 2016).

To better understand critical reflection as a form of social justice, Askeland and Fook (2009) think through the difference between critical thinking and critical reflection. Critical thinking is valued in progressive practice based on its adherence to principles derived from an awareness of the social and political bases of thought. Critical reflection enriches the practice of critical thinking through meaning making that employs direct experience, as well as through emotional support (Askeland and Fook, 2009). Drawing on critical social theory, Fook and Gardner (2007) describe five themes that define critical reflection:

- Power is present in practice in both structural and personal forms.
- An individual can participate in his or her own domination.
- Social change is both personal and social at the same time.
- Knowledge is socially constructed as well as empirical.
- Communication and dialogue are essential to practice.

Fook and Gardner (2007) and Irving (2012, 2014) combine postmodernism with critical reflection in order to question unified, linear, and developmental approaches to practice. They are aware of the link between power and knowledge so that one can deconstruct dominant discourses. When we reflect on new experiences, we create meaning that requires us to be open to changing our own guiding life principles and basic beliefs (Fook and Kellehear, 2010). Furthermore, from a social justice perspective, the analysis of power tied to social inequity can also lead to a change in our individual thinking and personal and social experiences. This awareness, at times, can lead to a feeling of personal power and transformation (Fook, 2014).

Through a critical reflection approach, one works from a social justice perspective that exists within a fluid frame. Justice is process as much as it is an endpoint of practice. Critically reflective practice enables the worker to think about theory, social context, and process all at once, and through it the worker can make links between individual and broader social relationships. If reflective practitioners examine their fundamental principles of practice, they can practice with an awareness that is underpinned by a social justice perspective based in values and meaning making (Gardner 2012).

Rather than apply principles of social justice from an abstract model, the critical reflective approach is a fluid process during which one works through justice concerns based on the constitution of the self. This reflection on and reconsideration of the constitution of the self is a crucial aspect of critical reflection. Aspects of critical reflection include a change in the self, the public presentation of that changed self, and the creation of new practice. This process leads to the important step of creating new discourses. Since discourse constitutes the possibilities of self and practice in the first place, such a change is profound. This radical rethinking of the self and discourse engages us in the reconstitution of social relationships (Duval and Béres, 2011; Fook, 2012, 2016; Healy, 2005; Mandell, 2008; Trevelyan et al., 2012; Witkin, 2017).

DISCUSSION

A reflective approach counters the tendency in social work practice and educational settings to be technique driven and prescriptive in nature. The practitioner and service user become aware of themselves through interaction with each other (Orcutt, 1990). The reflection on practice includes the lived experience of the individual, as well as the information gained through interaction (Moffatt, 1999b). There is a hopeful element to this practice, as it is based on the idea that when we become sensitive to tacit knowledge that draws from both subjective and objective sources, we begin to create new possibilities (Saleebey, 2013).

Schön's interpretive frame has been appealing to me as an educator, since it provides an approach to professional practice whereby students feel they are being offered something: a concrete form of thinking through practice. Most importantly, this interpretive frame for practice has allowed me to intimate to students that there are elements to practice that are unspeakable, elements that are filled with affect (Moffatt, 1999b).

At the same time, practice is far sadder and more complex than what can be dealt with in a classroom setting. For example, as an educator, one can only intimate the complexities of child abuse investigations to prepare a student for the cognitive and affective reactions to practice incidents. Not all modes of practice or shocks in relationships with service users can be categorized or anticipated. Nor can every affect or emotional interpersonal relationship be listed to enable a concrete practice to be offered to address the stimuli of direct practice. The open frame of reflective practice allows us to imagine there is something far worse or far better than we are prepared to discuss in class. At the same time, the students whose own identities are marginalized can think about what is not being fully addressed in the classroom.

It might be argued that Schön's belief that we construct work through our actions and resignification of our actions is similar to the postmodern discussions of the importance of signs and discourse in the construction of reality. But with his reliance on humanistic principles that suggest an unchangeable core to the self, he does not call for the radical reconstitution of the self that is proposed in social work literature. Social work theorists strengthen approaches to reflective practice by focusing on the constitution of the social worker's self. In this manner, they critically reflect on the nature of the self, as well as professional subjectivity.

If ethical professional practice or emancipatory self-development is thought of as solely a positive attribute of the professional, we are likely engaging in a form of self-surveillance and self-correction through the process of reflection (Bleakley 1999, 320). This form of self-correction may fall short of culturally and socially reconstituting practice and the social context. Instead, it is important that we engage in a form of social work practice whereby we reflect on how the self has changed in the midst of practice. We also must reflect on the fundamental bases for meaning.

Educators focused on reflective social work practice set a difficult task for students by asking them to make many changes in their direction of practice while also making changes to the self. We also ask them to engage in a type of *not knowing* by thinking outside dominant taken-for-granted discourses. All the cognitive and emotional risks that we demand students take are situated in the context of an ever-changing and precarious social and political environment. How do they retain a sense of stability and move through the process? One way might be to consider the psyche and consciousness in the context of social change. In the following chapter, I argue that the professor should consider the psyche of the students in order to advance both personal and social attachments.

3

REFLECTIVE PRACTICE AS A
FORM OF CONSCIOUSNESS

North American university classrooms exist within an image-saturated culture defined by commercial imagery. Media shape the daily experience of both students and educators. In spite of the pervasiveness and intrusive nature of commercial imagery, or perhaps because of its omnipresence, it has been difficult to imagine social work classroom relations that take media and commercial imagery into account. In this chapter, I situate my discussion in the context of social-construction approach to social work, which positions all practice in the social context. I then discuss the touchstone thinking of Paulo Freire. I pay particular attention to Freire's concept of *conscientization* as a form of reflection. Drawing on the thought of Julia Kristeva, I then discuss the capitalist context of image consumption and creation. I argue that Kristeva's theoretical concepts of *psychic space* and *subject-in-process* are useful for imagining how students and educators navigate contemporary life in light of its saturation by images and text. Both Freire and Kristeva link the psyche to the socioeconomic and political context. In this manner, they critically reflect on the nature of the self and professional subjectivity. They strengthen our approaches to reflective practice that focuses on the constitution of the social worker's self, as outlined in chapter 2. I offer an example of a reflective exercise that is meant to engage students in *psychic space*. In particular, I feel we might think about a contemporary form of consciousness based on reflection, the psyche, and meaning making that leads to the development of a politicized sense of self.

SOCIAL-CONSTRUCTION AND SOCIAL WORK

The social-constructionist approach to social work, based on the social origins of human affairs, is congruent with both Freire's concept of consciousness and Kristeva's interest in meaning making. The central importance of social relations in constructing a person's well-being is the starting point of a social-constructionist approach (Witkin, 2017). According to Witkin (2017), "We are born into a world of socially constructed beliefs and objects that are part of our lived experience" (2017, 26). Three key components of social construction are truth, language, and discourse. Social constructionists are less interested in what is proved to be true than in discovering the meaning of truth claims and how they function in social circumstances. The focus of social constructionism can either be on processes or on larger forces such as social discourses or institutions (Witkin, 2017).

Knowledge, from a social-constructionist perspective, is contingent on social, cultural, and historical conditions (Witkin, 2012a, 2017). Based on postmodern thought, the social-constructionist stance holds that there is no prior truth to lived experience, nor any prior concept of well-being (Irving 1999, 2014; Witkin, 2012a). In addition, as with the postmodern thought outlined in chapter 1, there is no transcendent knowledge claim or root to knowledge that can be discovered through the scientific method. Knowledge becomes present through the way that social institutions and social relations inscribe meaning (Irving, 2014; Witkin, 2012a, 2017). In particular, language and symbols constitute reality rather than reflect reality (Chambon, 1999; Irving, 1999; Witkin, 2012a). Since the social-constructionist paradigm is sensitive to the influence of social relations, it is necessarily relativist and nonprescriptive when addressing social change (Witkin 2012a, 2017). Such ideas about the source of truth are elaborated in chapter 4.

Because of the relativist nature of social construction, one definitive meaning of social construction does not exist. Rather, from the point of view of social construction, resemblances can be discussed across diverse social arrangements. Social arrangements are never given; rather, participants actively construct their world through everyday practices and interactions (Witkin, 2017). So, too, there is not a singular methodology or process to explain how a person or social circumstance is constructed. In other words, by reconstituting what we know, our differing formulations of knowledge lead to differing actions. Action can be accomplished through the reformulation of knowledge (Chambon, 1999; Irving, 1999; Witkin, 2012a). Through the social-construction approach to social work, educators are encouraged to take a reflective, critical stance toward the taken-for-granted (Witkin, 2012a).

.lr.sss.sssss

Care of the Self and Ascesis: Making the Self Present Through Autoethnography

Foucault (1988a) isolated historical practices associated with the care of the self. *Care of the self* is a social practice rather than a solitary exercise. In fact, institutional relations are put in place that ensure the activities devoted to the regimen of the self are present socially (Halperin, 1995; Tanke, 2009). Integral to the care of the self is a form of *ascesis*. According to Foucault, *ascesis* is "the work that one performs on oneself in order to transform oneself or make one appear" (1997a, 137).

The use of narrative opens a possibility for care of the self as a process of making one's self present (Ball and Olmedo, 2013; Foucault, 1997a). Through care of the self, we better understand the cultural and social meanings around the construction of self (Ball and Olmedo, 2013; Fook, 2014; Witkin, 2012a, 2014b). The exercise of making one's self present differs according to social and historical context (Tanke, 2009). Autoethnography is a contemporary means to engage in acesis or care of the self and to engage in meaning making about the self.

According to Witkin, autoethnography is "an approach to inquiry, as a process of knowledge production, as a practice, and as a useful tool for professional development that can increase self-awareness and sensitize practitioners to the constitutive aspects of social and cultural contexts" (2014a, 21). Rather than seeking or unveiling a truth, autoethnographers seek to enrich their understanding of personal, social, and cultural relationships (Witkin, 2014a). Autoethnography need not be confined to narratives that include plot and character development or are fully developed. It is an approach that explores the historical and cultural social processes leading to the subjectivity of the autoethnographer. The focus is on the person telling the story as both the object of the story and the subject or storyteller (Béres, 2014; Graham, 2017; Hyatt, 2014). The story is meant to prompt engagement and open a dialogue with the person hearing or reading the story (Witkin, 2014a).

In the social work classroom, we are socially and personally constructed through care of the self and by making one's self present in the context of interpersonal and institutional relations. Our subjectivity is constructed through the institutional and social demands of the university. By focusing on one's self through autoethnography, one can unveil "the implicit thinking involved in personal experience" (Fook, 2014, 125). This form of reflection connects the personal and social in a manner that leads to comprehension of social circumstances, which in turn allows for action (Fook, 2014). Fook (2014) argues for a reflexive approach to autoethnography that examines the multifaceted experience through a number of theoretical frameworks. Through critical reflection, it possible not only "to unearth fundamental assumptions that make a connection with social and cultural contexts, but to use this process to remake understandings of experience and to provide further (critical) guidelines for action" (Fook, 2014, 126). Since meaning does not transcend human relations, meaning making is accomplished through social interaction and social means (Hyatt, 2014). A means to influence the social context and transform social relationships is through a conscious reflection on the care of the self and autoethnography. I now turn to the complementary thought of Freire and Kristeva, who both take a social approach to the constitution of the psyche and think about how we construct our selves and make those selves present.

FREIRE AND CONSCIENTIZATION

Freire, born in Brazil in 1921, worked for many years on popular education in his native country. Freire, a professor of the history and philosophy of education at the University of Recife, was imprisoned after a Brazilian coup d'état in 1964 because of the subversive elements in his teaching. In 1970 he became special consultant in the Office of Education for the World Council of Churches in Geneva (Paulo Freire biography, n.d.). Since the 1970s, Freire (1970a, 1970b) has been a key theorist in the consideration of reflective practice and social work education. His concepts have been used widely in social work, community development, and pedagogy literature (see, for example, Burstow, 1991; Giroux, 1992; Hare, 2004; Koenig et al., 2017; Lee, 1999; Narayan, 2000; Rwomire and Radithokwa, 1996).

Freire (1970a, 1970b) argues against a banking style of education in favor of education that engages participants in the process of becoming aware of how they construct knowledge. He encourages his readers to think about broad social influences on marginalized communities. He does this by promoting an approach to education and community development in which social facilitators help oppressed people think through and become aware of how their social circumstances influence how they view the world. By engaging participants in knowledge creation, this method allows them to become agents of their own change (Freire 1970a, 1970b).

Freire (1970a, 1970b) is interested in both the psyche of the individual and the shared consciousness of oppressed communities. He ties the psyche to social relations by arguing that the subjective awareness of the oppressed is closely tied to the social structures of oppression. One of the consequences of oppression is the personal and psychic experience of dehumanization. Reflexive praxis that includes an awareness of social factors contributes to liberation from oppression through the rehumanization of oppressed subjects. This process involves helping oppressed people to perceive their oppression in a manner that leads to awareness, which in turn engages them in struggle on their own behalf. The oppressed person's social reality is unveiled and critically objectified in a way that leads to a reflective understanding of lived oppression. In short, developing critical awareness of one's social position through reflection leads to action (Freire, 1970a, 1970b).

Conscientization is based on reflection about the oppressive structures that create disadvantage. This critical awareness opens people to dialogue so that they can act together to change the situation (Burstow, 1991; Freire, 1970b). The oppressed work on the psychological process of becoming critically conscientized about their situation. Through conscientization, oppressed people work against their own silence, alienation, and internalized oppression (Freire, 1970b).

Freire's (1970b) focus on hegemony and oppression appeals to social workers and cultural workers who work with marginalized and disadvantaged groups. According to Freire, the oppressor's worldview blocks the oppressed from full social participation and thwarts their well-being. In fact, it is argued that the oppressed internalize the oppressor's view of them. In other words, the oppressed carry the oppressors' perception of them as if it were part of their embodied self (Burstow, 1991; Freire, 1970b). In order to empower people, one has to help them rid themselves of this state of "internalized oppression" through critical reflection.

85

While becoming conscientized, the oppressed become involved in the process of taking action in relation to oppressive social structures (Freire, 1970b). According to Freire, becoming aware of oppression through reflection is not adequate. The reflective process must lead to motivation among the oppressed to make social change. It is only through action that social reality changes and we are able to uncover social myths. Through action, the oppressed can engage in critical reflective dialogue about the nature and mechanisms of oppression (Freire, 1970b; Parada et al., 2010).

REFLECTION: THE LIMITS AND POSSIBILITIES OF FREIRE'S APPROACH

Giroux (1992) cautions North American educators against drawing on Freire as if his paradigm could provide a blanket interpretation of social relations and a replicable method across a variety of educational and social settings. Too often, Freire's educational approach is taken up as if it could be applied without reference to a particular time and place. In particular, educators should avoid taking up his work without acknowledging its importance as a decolonizing approach (Giroux, 1992). Still more troubling is when educators do not situate themselves in the educational process when applying Freire's approach (Giroux, 1992; S. Jackson, 2007).

S. Jackson (2007) argues that the tendency to use universalizing language and to conceive of the reality between the educator and the oppressed as a binary social construction is a shortcoming of Freire's paradigm. The social world cannot solely be constructed in binaries, such as the oppressed and the oppressor or those in favor of and those against systems of oppression. The postmodern and reflexive approaches to practice, outlined in chapters 1 and 2, suggest that social change is more variant and complex than these binaries (Irving, 1999; Pease, 2002; Pease and Fook, 1999; Todd, 2005).

I am left with a number of questions about Freire's work as applied in a North American postsecondary educational setting. Does the rush to solidarity and to action presuppose a unitary group? Does the move to action make invisible diversity within the oppressed group, and does it adequately deal with social tensions among the participants? Is it always necessary to move to action in our teaching about justice and oppression? Can reality and truth be objectified so that they can be externalized and viewed critically? Is there not always an outsider? In facilitating consciousness, are we working from a deficit model whereby the oppressed are characterized as not being fully aware? Another binary occurs when we associate silence with compliance and place it in opposition to action, which is inherently more just.

In spite of my misgivings, some of Freire's key concepts remain central to my approach to reflective teaching. Freire reminds us to be respectful of students' awareness and the knowledge of their own social reality. His reflective approach helps educators guide students to disrupt taken-for-granted norms and knowledge. I agree with the importance of a reflective dialogue whereby students hear each other's stories and critically reflect on their own experiences (Freire, 1970b). Freire's approach is strengthened by its interdisciplinary nature. His knowledge creation and cultural critique are tentative and ever changing and, in this manner, are congruent with the strengths of the postmodern approach to change as well as the thought of Donald Schön (Giroux, 1992).

Freire helps us to understand that the psychic terrain is informed by social relations. Like Freire, I believe that an educator can help students to understand the subjective experience of social alienation, leading them to better understand how to be agents of social change and act to change their circumstances. Furthermore, through the Freirean approach, we are reminded of the importance of bringing concepts of the unconscious into conscious reality so that they can be explored, interrogated, and reflected on (Harms Smith and Nathane-Taulela, 2015).

In the next section, I discuss the work of Kristeva as a contemporary form of reflective practice focused on consciousness. Her approach to consciousness allows for eccentricity and avoids the rush to solidarity. It is my contention that this approach to consciousness is particularly relevant to the media-saturated, commercial North American culture.

KRISTEVA AND THE PROBLEM OF CAPITALIST CULTURE AND IMAGES

Kristeva, like Freire, is interested in the psyche in the context of social influences. She is a psychoanalyst, writer, and professor emeritus at the University of Paris Diderot. She is doctor honoris causa at a number of universities in the United States, Canada, and Europe (Julia Kristeva: Texts, n.d.).

The effect of contemporary capitalist change is so profound, Kristeva argues, that it is redefining the nature of the social bond, as well as what it is to be human (Kristeva, 1995). According to Kristeva (2002c), as societies evolve, so do the selves we create and the psychological stresses with which we struggle. Mental health and personal well-being are not separate from our global urban centers. Rather, since the self is constructed in reaction to, and in relationship with, its social reality, new forms of mental health are created within the commercial context of urban capitalist settings (Kristeva, 1995).

Consumerist Global Culture

According to Kristeva (1995), the central purpose of global Western commercial culture has been the spread of consumerism. Because of the investment of global capital in major cities, such as New York, London, Paris, and Toronto, urban areas are becoming more sterile. Globalized media create cultures within city centers that are becoming indistinguishable from each other because of the replication of banal imagery. These urban centers have become the center of capitalist marketing, which has led to the multiplication of omnipresent imagery. This imagery has a reifying influence on the possible expressions of what it is to be human (Kristeva, 1995). Furthermore, because of the spread of global capital, the social and economic context of these urban centers is defined by the following factors:

- A high cost of living, which leads to precariousness
- Greater disparity between classes
- The spread of global commercial enterprises
- Heightened social divisions based on race, class, and gender (Kristeva, 1995)

Kristeva describes a scene common to many global metropolitan centers:

I am picturing a sprawling metropolis with glass and steel build-
ings that reach to the sky, reflect it, reflect each other, and reflect
you—a city with people steeped in their own image who rush
about with overdone make-up on and who are cloaked in gold,
pearls, and fine leather, while in the next street over, heaps of filth
abound and drugs accompany the sleep of the fury of the social
outcasts. (1995, 27)

I have become preoccupied both with the evident disparity
between people in the urban setting and with the spread of imagery, partially because of the setting in which I teach. I teach at
a university in the heart of downtown Toronto, very close to a
square that intentionally mimics Times Square. A number of
years ago, I had an office from which giant commercial billboards
and video screens could be viewed in the near distance. I then
began to notice the encroachment of consumer images and commercial videos all over the campus of the publicly funded university. On the way to work, I walk through this square with the
lived reality of drug use, homelessness, and poverty alongside
the hyperreality of video screens that flash images of thin people,
new clothes, movie clips, and holiday destinations. In combination, the advertisements create banks of imagery that present as
walls enclosing this large public space.

The culture of consumption has led to such an incursion of
commercial images in both private and public space (Kristeva,
1995). Kristeva (1995) describes two important features of commercial imagery: the images are fragmented and are viewed in
a piecemeal fashion, and the imagery comes at us at a frenzied
speed. She worries that the saturation of images in public spaces,
as well as the way they are experienced, leads to affective states

of distraction and agitation. At other times, people are soothed by commercial imagery because it helps them to avoid the tensions of the social sphere and to avoid facing the troubling interpersonal interactions and the social disparity so evident in the street (Kristeva, 1995).

The threats from these distractions run so deep as to interfere with the work of the psyche and the transformation of psychic life. People are distracted by commercial images that have the principal purpose of defining people as consumers. This distraction, in turn, prevents people from facing the psychic conflict that is created by having to confront social inequity (Kristeva, 1995). According to Kristeva, the images "foreshadow a humanity, one whose psychological conveniences will be able to overcome metaphysical anxiety and the need for meaning" (1995, 8).

A critical moment for me in the development of my awareness occurred when I was teaching in a classroom that faced a classic university quadrangle filled with trees and grass. While I was using the whiteboard, a student pointed out the reflection of a commercial video on the whiteboard in front of the classroom. This video was being projected on a commercial screen two blocks away. While working on the whiteboard, I had been unaware that I was competing with a decipherable image of a young, thin, white man and woman dressed in brand-name clothing. This ghostlike image, to me, was a metaphor for the incursion of global capital within the public sphere of the university classroom. I feel that the students and I have become so accustomed to such incursions and the saturation of images that we do not notice them. I began to wonder how this onslaught of commercial imagery in public space was affecting my psyche and the psyche of my students. I also began to wonder how commercial media and its imagery influence the social relations of the classroom and my approach to pedagogy.

More recently, I have become a convert to social media. I now join the behavior of some of my students at break during class to check Facebook, Twitter, Gmail, or Instagram. This provides a way to remove myself from the possibilities and tensions of the classroom for a few minutes. Social media offer me a voluntary distraction from the tensions of class, but they also involve me with the imagery that agitates me. In these few moments, I scroll through advertisements of custom-built homes, tailored shirts, all-inclusive holidays, and the like, in addition to the noncommercial images posted by members of my social networks. It is my contention that this form of agitation leads to anxiety and stress, which only further emphasizes that we are in a time of precariousness, as outlined in chapter 1.

Threats to Meaning Making

According to Kristeva and Spire (2003), the replication of global images disrupts the process of singular and creative representation of the self that is made possible only through imaginative engagement. A consumerist approach to symbols, and the storing of information, results in a narrowed space to explore meaning (Kristeva, 2002c). In other words, the banality and the lack of singular, unique representations in Western capitalist culture restrict the dialectic of meaning making. We are at risk of understanding ourselves and meaning making within a narrow, unimaginative discourse of commerce (Kristeva and Spire, 2003). As mentioned earlier, this narrowing of discourse is accompanied by a dulling of our reaction to the sociocultural environment within which we exist (Kristeva and Spire, 2003).

The superficial (closed, sterile, and complete) and dreamlike (fragmented and speeded up) nature of these images confines the symbolic discourse that we can draw on to connect with our bodies and other people (Kristeva, 1995). The images trouble meaning making and the constitution of the self because of their nature. We can never be fully present to such contained images (Kristeva, 2000; Schroeder, 2005).

Contemporary capitalist culture presents two threats to the growth of the psyche, which can only be accomplished through deep reflective thought associated with meaning making. The first threat to personal growth is the widespread distraction of banal imagery, described earlier (Kristeva, 1995). The second threat is the rise of scientific knowledge that privileges the biological interpretation of mental health above all other interpretations (Kristeva, 1995; Witkin, 2012a, 2014a). Overreliance on interventions such as pharmacology poses a risk to personal and social change when the simple act of taking a pill becomes the most efficient manner of dealing with mental health. Both these threats are characterized by a focus on efficiency and an oversimplification of remedies related to mental health. Pharmacology and capitalist commercial imagery replace the search for healthy expressions of the self with action defined by either distraction or efficiency (Kristeva, 1995). In this manner, efficiency, which is congruent with the political power strategies of neoliberalism defined in chapter 1, has a direct effect on the constitution of the psyche.

With the restricted range of commercial imagery, the incoherence of images that arises from the quickness with which they are presented, and the fragmented quality of their presentation, it is more difficult to engage in the interplay of the semiotic and the symbolic necessary to meaning making (Kristeva, 2002a; Kristeva and Spire, 2003). In the next section, I discuss possibilities for allowing for imaginative subjectivity that leads to meaning making.

Psychic Life

According to Kristeva (2002b), meaning making requires both the semiotic and the symbolic. This psychoanalytic approach takes into account both biology and social relations to develop an interpretation of cultural affairs (Kristeva, 2002b). All meaning making is possible because of the tension and the dialectic movement between the process of the semiotic and the stasis of the symbolic (Oliver, 2002). The semiotic is that part of the meaning-making process that is based in drives and affect that exist before, or outside, image creation (Kristeva, 2002b). The semiotic is expressed through melodic and rhythmic articulations rather than through signifiers (Kristeva, 2002b; Oliver, 2002).

At the same time, meaning making requires complementary work related to the symbolic—that is, the linking of signs or signifiers together in a series so that they exist in a structure. The symbolic is signification that is associated with judgment and organization. Language and symbols possess an underlying driving force (semiotic) but also have organizing structures and principles that make communication possible (symbolic) (Oliver, 2002). The semiotic necessarily interferes with the arrangement and logic of language and the organization of the symbolic

(Kristeva, 2002b; Oliver, 2002). The semiotic is a process, while the symbolic is static (Kristeva, 2002b).

Psychic Spaces

Both Freire and Kristeva argue that students and educators create meaning by exploring and creating their own images and language. Kristeva, however, offers a framework for understanding a contemporary form of consciousness raising. According to her, we require a *psychic space* in order to be involved in meaning making. This psychic space is the space in which we find meaning through connections to our body and one another (Oliver, 2002).

According to Kristeva, the psyche remains "an implacable enigma. As a structure of meaning, the psyche represents the bond between the speaking being and the other, a bond that endows it with therapeutic and moral value. Furthermore, by rendering us responsible for our bodies, the psyche shields us from biological fatalism and constitutes us as speaking entities" (1995, 4).

Psychic spaces are spaces for love, attachment, and symbolic creation, or in other words, the interplay between the semiotic and the symbolic (Kristeva, 2000). In the psychic space of personal transformation, we can allow for two seemingly contradictory processes to occur: the experience of longing for attachment (Kristeva, 2002b) and the achievement of a distance from attachment that is adequate to form a speaking subject and "to accede to language" (Kristeva, 2002b, 337). This form of consciousness may be eccentric and unique to each person but is also responsible to the social body (Oliver, 2002). Change is possible in psychic space in spite of the powerful social and cultural influences, such as commercial imagery and global capitalism, that can hinder personal transformation (Kristeva, 2002c). Pietroni, in discussing the profession of social work, similarly argues that we need to "provide a containing environment in which individual practitioners are given the opportunity of recovering or establishing creative individual thought" (1995, 48).

The Subject in Process

The speaking subject (the human) is always engaged in a precarious process of constructing the self and creating symbols of meaning (Oliver, 2002). The speaking subject can never be fully developed or completely unified (Oliver, 2002). Human desire in a contemporary setting, according to Kristeva, is to be thought of as a form of questioning rather than as a calculation. Furthermore, at the borders, this form of constant questioning refers to the semiotics that lie beyond reason (Kristeva, 2002b). Because of the dialectic at the heart of symbol creation, signifiers are indeterminate and unknowable. Therefore, Kristeva proposes a social and political project that involves "an endless probing of appearances" through "permanent questioning that characterizes psychic life" (2002c, 120). This project is meant to put reflective processes in play that work in tension with the unquestioning superficiality of contemporary capitalist imagery that disengages, isolates, and dulls both the senses and intellectual capability (Kristeva, 1995). Reflection from this point of view is necessarily endless, with no finality possible (Kristeva, 2002c).

Kristeva (2002b) argues for a continual revolution of self, a practice of personal and social change that entails the search for meaning through ongoing interrogation and reflection, which frees us for social change. One manner to work toward justice engages us in an ongoing examination of our doubts, which we usually avoid in our desire to be confident and definite in our political and intellectual lives (Derrida, 1997). This ongoing examination of doubt is akin to Kristeva's call for constant questioning and reflection as an ongoing political process and the supple forms of justice proposed by the social work theorists discussed in chapter 2 (Duval and Béres, 2011; Fook, 2012; Mandell, 2007; Trevelyan et al., 2012).

REFLECTION: THE LIMITS AND POSSIBILITIES OF KRISTEVA'S THOUGHT

A strength of Kristeva's thought is that she has "positioned herself on the threshold between aesthetics and politics, signification and materiality, the psychic and the social" (Margaroni, 2007, 793). In addition, she imagines "a discursive and conceptual system where thinking qua innovation and beginning is predicated on the ability to cross . . . familiar fixed boundaries" (Margaroni, 2007, 793). It is this strength, however, that has led to critiques of her approach. Since her sense of revolt focuses on the psychic change of the individual, it might be limited to addressing change in the person's subjectivity within the existing system rather than a change of the system as a whole (Brandt, 2001). In fact, it has been argued that in her focus on the intimate, as well as her personal psychic maladies, she has shifted from an examination of structures of oppression (Margaroni,

2007). In addition, there have been questions about how personal subjectivity and personal experimentation can have a direct relationship to social, political transformation. Can intimate revolt and reflection be characterized as similar to political or social revolt? Can familial relations, as imagined through psychoanalysis, be analogous to broader social relations (Margaroni, 2007)?

Furthermore, Kristeva's thought has been critiqued because she does not acknowledge that psychoanalysis and the key concepts on which she draws are situated in a cultural context. By not openly discussing the context and assumptions of the psychoanalytic approach, one avoids considering the masculinist assumptions behind concepts such as drive, affect, and the unconscious (Margaroni, 2007). Similarly, in social work, Healy (2005) argues that psychological theories have assumed a taken-for-granted quality. Some fundamental key concepts in social work, such as mutuality in relationship, are borrowed from the "psy sciences" without consideration of the social and cultural context within which they have been created. Nor do social workers think through the social nature of some psychological concepts as they are tied to institutional, cultural, and historical context.

In spite of these limitations, if educators are sensitive to students' need for psychic space, students can begin to reflect on psychic and social relationships (Oliver, 2002). It seems to me that psychic spaces might be formed in the classroom to allow students to engage in complex meaning making in the context of media-saturated culture. I imagine these spaces as three-dimensional, in contrast to the two-dimensional commercial imagery that either is speeded up and fractured or already has its meaning in place. Within these psychic spaces, both students and educators make sense of social and psychic worlds by combining desires for attachment with endless combinations of symbolic creation (Kristeva, 2000). Through psychic space, students and educators can reengage with their own imaginative creativity. They can also encounter the unknown in relation to themselves (Kristeva and Spire, 2003).

I am arguing here for a form of consciousness that differs from, but is not necessarily contradictory to, Freire's process of conscientization. Whereas Freire's sense of consciousness is assumed to be shared and leading to action, Kristeva's conscious development is eccentric, autonomous, and ever changing. In both cases, the psyche is socially constituted. I argue that in North American image-saturated society, there is a need to retrieve a space where people can engage in both attachment and symbol creation to create meaning for themselves. I now turn to how this meaning is made present in the classroom.

STUDENT ENGAGEMENT
IN PSYCHIC SPACE

Through my exposure to the thought of Kristeva, I now envision a classroom where guided processes for each student are as important as didactic learning. The classroom pedagogical process needs to allow for psychic space. The processes can be imagined as a manner for students to create meaning by making themselves present socially through ascesis and autoethnography. We can imagine how to work with students who are attempting to grapple with their sense of professional and personal self within contemporary culture by considering Kristeva's emphasis on the role of the psyche. In order to do this work, classrooms can be imagined as a space for a series of guided processes. How do we imagine and provide a space for students so that they can probe the symbolic environment to better understand how their psyches are influenced by their social context? If students are to use only technological means to create symbols about the other, then they are likely to be wrapped in a type of anxiety.

One element of the classroom process involves the intrapsychic work of the student, which occurs while the student is tied to social relationships. This intrapsychic work and social awareness can be coupled to create meaning for the student. Another element of the classroom process is for the student to reveal both attachment or drive and his or her own symbols. In other words, students perform the following acts:

- Work through attachment and meaning.
- Reveal attachment and symbol creation socially.
- Experience changing social situations that are reactions to revealing the self in the classroom.
- Engage in ongoing reflection about the self and social dynamics both within the class and outside the classroom.

At the same time, professors are involved in their own reflection; they are engaged in their own form of ascesis while remaining aware of the social process of the classroom. The teaching process involves a number of acts performed by the educator, including the following:

- Constantly frame and reframe the process of the class.
- Nurture a space for personal reflection.
- Withdraw from surveillance of the student.
- Accede the professorial voice.
- Intervene in the social sphere when necessary.

- Be aware of one's own ascesis as an educator.
- Encourage discussion and support risk.

This type of ongoing professorial commitment to reflective process supports personal change that can have social consequences. When students reveal some aspects of the self in the classroom, semiotic and symbolic reconstruction of the psyche can be attempted. This form of ascesis also allows for previously unforeseen relations to be imagined. A reflective process can be put into play whereby students can become aware of and respond to others' reactions to themselves as *subjects in process*. Also, by being a "speaking agent" who creates language and symbols, a student can challenge the context of our sanitized and problematic consumer-driven social structure.

By reflecting on their evolving presence in the classroom, the students and the educator can imagine the multiplicity of relations within which they are embedded. They can also reflect on the multiplicity of relations that might be created (Foucault, 1997a; Irving and Young, 2002). For some marginalized students, this may be their first experience of ascesis, since the social context within which the classroom exists may not have been supportive of their subjective engagement in the past (Baileyugu et al., 2000; Moffatt, 2001b; Pon et al., 2011). In this manner, psychic space and the subject in process become political, since the students and professor begin to reimagine social relations in a manner that allows for the invention of social relations that do not exist (Foucault, 1997a).

The ability to provide a space for students to work through the process of meaning making is challenged by increases in class size, which encourage the professor to impart knowledge through lectures rather than in dialogue with the students. The structure of such a classroom, with the students facing a professor and watching a multimedia lecture, does not aid in learning about the semiotic. Furthermore, technology that complements teaching through online formats also encourages a didactic approach to teaching. While technologies of teaching have liberated the professor to use video clips, photographic imagery, and interactive tools and text, if we use these tools, we run the risk of inviting the students to experience yet more fragmented imagery.

I have in the past imagined the solution to this problem of the dialectic of the self for social work students to be one of interpersonal learning. I felt that classrooms needed to be smaller and that I needed to be in direct interaction with the students, or that the students needed to learn in dyads and in conversation to understand how to deal with both the semiotic and the symbolic. That is, I believed that through dyadic exercises, they could think about how they construct knowledge about each other and how they feel about each other. I still believe that the best way to learn in the human services is through interpersonal meaning making (Miehls and Moffatt, 2000; Moffatt and Miehls, 1999).

At the same time, there may be ways that one can use technology to think through meaning making in an image-saturated society. In fact, the advent of the internet, the growth of information technology, and the plethora of images offer a rich resource for thinking through symbolic meaning making. I have become increasingly interested in helping students to consider the symbolic culture of mass media and consumerist capital. It seems that there are two aspects to this type of learning. One is becoming literate in symbols that may be taken for granted. The other is the introduction of the semiotic into the creation of meaning.

As mentioned in chapter 1, I have invited students to consider the constraints and limitations of the neoliberal and new managerial approaches to social work education while also inviting them to explore topics that are tied to the marginalization of people. By the end of the term, I hope that they understand the precariousness of all people but are also aware of the specific types of precariousness that arise from differences in race, gender, class, ability, and sexuality. In addition, I encourage them to think about their attachments, as well as how symbols support and contradict their sense of self.

In the absence of the process defined earlier, which includes psychic space, the self in process, ascesis, and autoethnography, the multiple commercial images we are exposed to can lead to the extinction of singular representations of our selves. The dire consequence of the lack of such a process is "the absence of any social and political project" (Kristeva and Spire, 2003, 22). Most importantly, the dialectic between the semiotic and symbolic is threatened, and the imaginative act of self-expression is therefore put at risk. Most threatened are the important elements of social bonding that are associated with semiotic drives. This has implications for the classroom if educators are attempting to create a space for reflective practice that leads to the reinvigoration of imagination in relation to both the self and the social. Through our pedagogy, we can seek to carve out the freedom for creative, imaginative self-expression, knowing full well it will involve a reflective process that is, at times, tense, anxious, and questioning.

The educator then needs to be aware of the institutional practices in place in the classroom that allow for the care of the self and ultimately for the subject in process. The narrative is understood through reflection, and that reflection involves thinking about a process that includes both attachment and symbol creation. As is the case with the subject in process, ascesis is never finished, and the self is never complete. In social work, if students are able to take an autoethnographic approach to their practice, they may be able to explore meaning making through psychic space.

REFLECTION: WIKIPEDIA—
ATTACHMENT AND SYMBOL CREATION
FOR THE INTERNET

Librarian Diane Granfield and I designed an exercise involving the online platform Wikipedia in order to involve students in a process that makes them aware of both attachment and symbol creation. Students were given an assignment that involved either rewriting an article or creating a new article on Wikipedia. The students were asked to choose an article, or topic area, related to marginalization in the broadest sense of the term. They also were encouraged to pick a topic or population with which they are personally or subjectively engaged. The students were asked to summarize and critique the article in terms of form, content, and discourse. The overall purpose of the assignment was to expand students' awareness of, and skill in, critically analyzing the production of knowledge about marginalized groups, particularly knowledge mediated through the internet. It was also meant to engage students in imagining audiences for their symbol creation, as well as reflecting on their attachment to others.

Wikipedia, launched in 2001, is an online encyclopedia or a conversational technology (Granfield and Moffatt, 2009). Wikipedia is "an effort to create and distribute a free encyclopedia of the highest possible quality to every single person on the planet in their own language" (Wikipedia: About, 2018). As the dominant platform in online searches for information, it has become a major source of contemporary knowledge. Anyone with access to a computer and the requisite technical skills can contribute to Wikipedia. Each person who does is engaged in a self-conscious collaboration (Granfield and Moffatt, 2009). The encyclopedia is made up of entries, called articles, written by mostly anonymous volunteer participants from around the world. Entries are moderated by volunteer editors. Since Wikipedia does not contain any original research, content is not original. In fact, content must be verifiable through reference to other sources (Wikipedia: About, 2018).

Wikipedia is based on five pillars:

- It is an encyclopedia.
- It is free content that anyone can use, edit, and distribute.
- It is written from a neutral point of view.
- Editors should treat each other with respect and civility.
- Wikipedia has no firm rules. (Wikipedia: Five Pillars, 2018)

Wikipedia provides a starting point for students to think about the links between power, knowledge, and discourse. Articles are meant to document and explain major points of view in an impartial tone. The weight of the point of view depends on its prominence in the entry. Furthermore, the site is meant to describe issues and provide information rather than advocate for a particular point of view. Articles are not provided for the purpose of debating differing points of view. In some instances, multiple points of view are presented, as long as they are described with accuracy and in context and as long as there is no attempt to determine the best view or the truth. In other articles, one sole point of view is presented if it is the one that is well recognized. All articles cite reliable, authoritative sources to ensure that their accuracy is verifiable (Granfield and Moffatt, 2009; Wikipedia: Five Pillars, 2018). Personal experience, interpretation, and opinions are not welcome on Wikipedia (Wikipedia: Five Pillars, 2018). The neutral point of view is a departure for discussions about both discourse and subjectivity.

The Wikipedia assignment is a good exercise in symbol creation because of the multiple levels of discourse in the design of the platform. Wikipedia's neutral point of view illustrates the bias in favor of technology and technical knowledge. Students often struggle with the limits of the neutral point of view, most notably with respect to gender bias in entries. Also, Wikipedia provides active links to other sources of information. These links encourage lateral thinking rather than deep thinking in knowledge construction. Furthermore, the limits of discourse and symbol creation are evident through the absence of certain entries on Wikipedia. Students can think through the multiple constraints on thinking (or epistemes) while making themselves present on the site and in the classroom.

For the Wikipedia assignment, students are encouraged to pick a topic close to their heart—about a community they belong to, about an issue tied to their subjective experience, or about an experience they have had. In short, they are encouraged to explore topics about people that involve a sense of attachment and affect. The attachment also occurs between group members who have chosen a topic with a shared emotional attachment. Although students are not required to be members of the communities chosen for study, social work students often identify with the marginalized population, community, or person they seek to represent. For example, a group of single mothers rewrote a Wikipedia entry on motherhood, a group of black women focused on antiblack racism, and a group of queer-identified students of multiple genders rewrote the entry on the word *queer*. The group work is intended to help students work through a form of Freirean conscientization, thus leading to some shared meaning, but more importantly, it is meant to engage students in symbol creation, attachment, and discourse to enable them to think through Kristeva's principles of psychic space.

Other topics that students choose include the killing of black men by police officers in the United States, the disappearance of Aboriginal women in Canada, rave cultures, online gaming, the WorldStarCandy/WorldStarHiphop website, domestic violence, Tamils in India, and the Mississauga ancestral Aboriginal lands. The students are then engaged in the exercise of creating language and symbols or discourse about each of these topics. By reconstructing discourse, the students are, in fact, disrupting the passive subjection of their selves as students and people. They become knowledge creators rather than information consumers.

When students present their reconstructed Wikipedia entries to the classroom, they are engaged in discourse creation that influences both the online community and the classroom. In many cases, the students are also involved in form of autoethnography or ascesis, having gone through an exercise of attachment and image creation. Discourse in this manner becomes productive (Butler, 1990, 1993). By engaging in a practice of education and a discourse that is repeated in the classroom, the students and I make possible subjectivities or subjects in process, often informed by gender, race, class, sexuality, and ability, that then influence the interpersonal and social politics of the classroom. The students become agents not only of knowledge creation but also of discursive interventions that may contribute to social change by challenging the hegemonic, taken-for-granted knowledge both in the classroom and online.

Beyond the goals just described, I also hope to support students in the creation of consciousness through exploration in psychic space. Through the work on Wikipedia, the students interact with both written and visual symbols. Attachments develop between group members but also to the population being discussed and to imagined communities. It is more important to me that students have an affective attachment to the topic than that groups be consistent in terms of composition and size. Also, topic or entries must be self-selected and voluntary. In addition to exploring discourse, epistemes, and knowledge creation, the students explore symbol creation and attachment and are therefore working on the psyche.

DISCUSSION

In this chapter I have focused on reflection on the context of meaning making in an image-saturated culture. I situated the discussion within the social-constructionist point of view, which encourages a form of autoethnography. I considered the thought of Paulo Freire, Julia Kristeva, and Michel Foucault in order to think through how a student's psyche can be engaged in processes of social change and social justice. I outlined some key concepts from each author, including Freire's dehumanization

108

and conscientization, Kristeva's psychic space and self in process, and Foucault's ascesis or making the self present. I argued that the professor should take a reflective stance to teaching that is more akin to guided process than the didactic teaching of information. In the reflective stance, the professor is aware of the students' need both for quiet time or space to develop attachment and for social space to experiment with symbol creation.

I have discussed technology in a variety of ways thus far. These include conceptualizing it as a worldview that values reductive thinking, and the application of knowledge for technical practice over critical thinking. I have also discussed technology as a form of neoliberal governance tied to the information economy. It has been discussed in this chapter as a means to spread commercial imagery, as well as a mediated discourse that allows students to engage in questions of attachment and image creation. In the next chapter, I think through ways to imagine the technology that is present in the classroom in terms of both hardware and software.

4

THE SOCIAL WORK CLASSROOM
AS A PLAY OF DYNAMIC
ELEMENTS

Du
uring the 1990s, in an undergraduate social work
class entitled Identity and Diversity, I asked students
to take a few minutes to talk about some aspect of their
identities. I often asked students to speak to their identities as
early as the second class of term. After I explained how a person's personal and social identity is socially constructed around
factors such as race, gender, sexual orientation, ethnicity, and
class, I invited each student to share with the rest of the class a
significant aspect of his or her identity formation. My intention
was to help create consciousness for students about the importance of identity, especially identities that are normally marginalized. I also intended to open a discursive terrain that made each
of their identities present for consideration and discussion. Students in that progressive social work program were already aware
of their identities from class discussions in other courses and
often responded first from the point of view of their marginal
social location. Students who did not perceive themselves as situated in a socially marginal position often were apologetic about
their self-perception as privileged people. I thought I was involved
in a form of consciousness raising. But now I am uncertain how

well this exercise helped students to think through the construction of identity in a productive manner, especially in light of the need for psychic space, as outlined in chapter 3. Perhaps the type of response a student offered to the request to claim an identity was tied to the care of self, as defined in chapter 3, expected in a progressive, public social work program.

At present, in 2018, I find the notion of a professor raising the consciousness of students to be suspect. Rather, I imagine my role, discussed in the previous chapter, as one of an educator who supports students to work on their psychic structure in the context of social relations. Upon reflection, I believe that in the past I was trying to illustrate the importance of multiple subjectivities in the classroom, yet I took a veiled, neutral stance in terms of both my own identity and its relationship to the students. It also was not clear to the students what my response to their identity claims would be (Moffatt, 2004, 2012c). Was I judging their response according to merit (Moffatt, 2006)? At the same time, I wonder whether the exercise was somewhat ritualistic for some students who had declared their identities in other classes in order to meet the expectations and gain the approval of their progressive professors. For students who claimed dominant identities, part of the "ritual" may at times have included the "appropriate" emotional reaction of shame, remorse, or anger (Heron, 2005). Perhaps the exercise required a richer autoethnographic approach that helped students think through how they were announcing their identities in the context of a classroom containing conflicting discourses.

I feel I was being somewhat dogmatic by assuming I could create consciousness about student identities. To engage in this exercise suggests that I, the educator, with my unitary identity, have a heightened awareness about identity compared with my students, which enables me to tell others how their identities are socially constructed and instruct them in the way to reveal identity respectfully.

In this chapter, I continue to argue for the importance of an awareness of identity in the classroom. It makes sense, in light of the social work knowledge outlined in chapter 3, that I continue to think about the importance of discussing the self in the classroom. But I now attempt to rethink the concept of identity by drawing on Gilles Deleuze and Félix Guattari's concepts of the *planar*, *assemblage*, and *rhizomatic change*. By employing these concepts, our thinking about pedagogy can shift from being solely focused on the student as a unitary individual to also taking into account other components of the classroom, such as the presence of the educator and technology in the classroom.

THE SELF AND IDENTITY CLAIMS IN THE CLASSROOM

When asked about identity in the 1990s, students in my urban classroom mostly spoke to the ethnicity of their families, such as Jamaican, Portuguese, Italian, South Asian, and Chinese. While most students spoke of ethnic identities as cultural identities, some students spoke of those ethnic identities as if they were racial identities. Surprisingly, though social work classrooms are made up almost entirely of women, only a few of the students spoke of gender in terms of their identity formation. In the late 1990s, I had not yet had a student who was prepared to speak openly of matters of sexual orientation as early as the second class of term (Moffatt, 2001b). The disclosures are different in 2018, when, depending on context, the content of the course, and the method of my introduction, some students may speak openly about race and sexuality very early on in the course.

Gender discussions, in particular, have a broader reach when I teach now. In the past, gender mostly seemed to be addressed when cisgender women discussed their awareness of social relations that disadvantaged them. Currently, discussions of gender have a much broader scope, including some transgender, gender fluid, and transsexual students openly declaring their gender identities (Pyne, 2016). The topic of sexual identity has opened up as well, with students prepared to discuss questioning, wondering, queer, and bisexual identities in addition to gay and lesbian identities. At times, those whose identities are loosely categorized as queer include those who eschew labels about their sexual orientation (LaSala, 2013).

The changing claims of identity support the exercise of encouraging students to speak from the point of view of identity; it continues to be a useful exercise in creating a discursive terrain that accommodates the multiplicity of identity. Speaking identity makes present sexual, racial, and gendered discourses that then become part of the expectations of the classroom (Moffatt, 2001b). In addition, the declaration of identity in the classroom makes visible identities that may have been unspeakable in the past (Butler, 1993). I learn about new possibilities as students declare identities I had not yet imagined. Speaking identities allows both me and the students to become aware of how identity claims have changed over time (Moffatt, 2004). Identity claims in the classroom are most important to me because they are a means to make the self present, or to engage in ascesis, in the classroom. By declaring an identity, students can become aware of the self and subjectivity through direct experience of the changing context of language and power relations in the classroom. Foucault (1997a, 1997b) offers a useful rubric for imagining how the self is constituted in the classroom. He discusses four modalities or technologies that make the self possible, including the following:

- Language and discourse, including language and sign systems
- Technologies of production, which allow people to produce control and convert things
- Technologies of self, which are tied to how people make themselves present as subjects and make sense of their subjectivity
- Technologies of power, which concern the way individuals are influenced and the nature of socially constructed states of domination (Foucault, 1997a, 1997b; Sirotich et al., 2012)

The modes by which a student can become a subject and express the self are defined in the classroom by the interplay of all these technologies (Sirotich et al., 2012).

Strategies of Power

Building on the previous discussion of Foucauldian concepts of power in chapters 1 and 3, in this section I discuss how power is manifested in the classroom. As mentioned in chapter 1, every relationship is also a relationship of power. In a broader context, power is the complex strategies of relations within a society (Gordon, 1980; Kritzman, 1988). The power of the educator is not defined by the educator's social stature alone. Neither is power a principle of individual character or an unfathomable property that one possesses (Foucault, 1988b). Because power does not exist in a substantive form, neither does it exist in an institutional or social-structural form that is abstracted from the interplay of strategic relationships (Gordon, 1980). As previously discussed, in the contemporary contest, techniques of power are elaborated so that they are continuous and uninterrupted but at the same time adaptable and individualized (Foucault, 1980d). Within such an economy of power, power is distributed widely rather than concentrated solely at points of privilege (Foucault, 1979).

The contemporary form of power is advantageous to those exercising it because it can be exerted on the smallest element in the social body—that is, at the point of microinterventions. The exercise of power has become more efficient. Economic and political costs are minimized, whereas the effectiveness of the exercise of power had been enhanced (Foucault, 1979, 1980d). Although the educator can, and likely does, engage in overt displays of power, he or she also engages in many strategic and widespread uses of power in the classroom that are less obvious. At times, the professor may exercise power through microinterventions with unintended consequences or without full awareness that a physical or speech act is an exercise of power.

A more precise reading of Foucault's concepts of power and knowledge has helped me to better understand the social work classroom setting. When the classroom is understood in terms of the links between power, knowledge, and language, one of the purposes of reflection for both the students and professor is to consider how they are implicated in dangerous practices. It seems to me that students, particularly in a practice-oriented course, need to consider how they link the knowledge of others

116

with the exercise of power (Foucault 1980a, 1980b; Heron, 2005; Rossiter, 2000).

Arguably, the various strategies constructed by me and the students with respect to the interlinking of power and knowledge are limitless. The multiple ways in which we can construct truths about each other suggest the need to microanalyze specific relations in order to unveil how knowledge of the other is constructed (Foucault 1980a, 1980b, 1988a). At the same time, in the past, my pedagogical position has been that students need to be prompted to consider how they both consciously and unconsciously exercise practices of privilege. Yet professors are also implicated by their presence in the room and engagement in the exercise of power and knowledge (Moffatt, 2004). This continues to be a useful form of pedagogy and reflection; however, it is not enough.

The exercise of asking students to claim an identity may fail by suggesting that the self is a unified entity with a consciousness that is aware of itself. In fact, the self is historic and contingent on the interplay of technologies (Chambon, 1999; Foucault, 1997b; Irving, 1994; Sirotich et al., 2012). Since the self is constructed through a number of institutional and discursive frames and operations of power (Chambon, 1999), including new managerialism, technology, and neoliberalism, as outlined in chapter 1 (Moffatt et al., 2016), the self is not necessarily a unified entity (Chambon, 1999; Irving, 1999, 2014). Consciousness, too, is shifting and open to continuous change and reflection rather than being unitary (Kristeva, 2002c; Martinez-Brawley, 2001).

Also, with the various modalities or technologies of the self outlined earlier, the self may be constituted in any number of forms with a wide variety of states of self-awareness. So my past exercise of asking students to reveal identity is only as effective as our shared awareness of how each student influences and is influenced by the technologies of discourse, production, power, and self within the classroom. At worst, the claim of an identity could obscure the complexities of subjectivity, identity constitution, ascesis, and the presence of the self in the classroom.

Discipline and Examination

Within the strategies of power mentioned earlier, various techniques and procedures are developed that are useful in the coercion of people's bodies. Discipline is one such strategy within the contemporary economy of power. Examination is another strategy of power (Foucault, 1979). These two strategies seem to be particularly relevant to the classroom, where the professor is in charge of sorting students according to merit in order to assign grades (Moffatt, 1999a, 2006).

Discipline is "the specific technique of power that regards individuals both as objects and as instruments of its exercise" (Foucault, 1979, 170). Through the act of discipline, one distinguishes, separates out, and sorts individual bodies from the mass of humanity (Foucault, 1979). Discipline operates through minor procedures and modes, and the success of disciplinary power is determined by the manner with which it becomes operational through simple techniques.

Upon reflection, it seems that an educator asking students to speak their identities is suspect of exercising discipline that functions as a calculated economy of power. Certainly, prompting students to speak identity is an exercise that leads to the sorting of individuals within the classroom. Such a procedure may enhance atomization and docility at the personal level (Foucault, 1979). The declaration of identity may be one of those simple techniques that are part of the disciplinary exercise of power. By asking for the students to speak their identities, I am coconstituting them in the classroom to help make sense of my strategies of power. In listening to the student's declaration of identity, I need to be cautious in how I sort the student from his or her classmates and find a categorical approach to identity. This atomization and categorization of students can allow me to develop meticulous methods to ensure that each student fits within the social machinery that is the classroom (Foucault, 1979). I need to be aware that asking students to declare aspects of their identities is the first stage of the disciplinary exercise of categorizing and shaping students.

Furthermore, the examination, a technology central to education, is an instrument of disciplinary power. It combines hierarchical observation with a normalizing judgment. It is distinguished by its simplicity and effectiveness (Foucault, 1979). Foucault elaborates on the character of the examination: "It is a normalizing gaze, a surveillance that makes it possible to qualify, to classify and to punish. It establishes over individuals a visibility through which one differentiates them and judges them" (1979, 184). The effect of the examination is the subjection of interrogated peoples so that they become objects of measurement and study. Within this simple technique of examination lies a profound interrelationship of knowledge and power. The examination makes it possible to collect and constitute knowledge at the point of interaction. The specific details of the micro practice create the possibility of knowledge; in this manner, practice and knowledge take on a political nature. The examination implies an entire domain of knowledge related to the specific exercise of power (Foucault, 1979).

The white, cisgender, male professor who asks students to speak their identities continues to stand in observation of the students (Moffatt, 2004, 2012c). There is a danger that I am involved in a moral judgment of how students declare their identities, no matter how much I wish to introduce neutrality to the exercise. I might judge that an identity claim has been introduced in a troubling fashion that invites dissension and social tension in the classroom. For example, I have distrusted some white students' declarations of overly romanticized rural or small-town identities characterized by the shared values of acceptance in the small-town setting. At other times, I judge whether students introduce their identities with an adequate level of humility. If a student identity claim is delivered with some self-reflective humility, I suspect my categorization becomes more favorable. As I examine student identities, I make judgments about them and I start to construct knowledge about each student and the classroom as a whole. It could be argued that I am asking them to introduce their subjective selves into the classroom to make them present for discipline, examination, and correction.

I now believe that in calling on students to declare an identity in the classroom, one needs to proceed with caution to avoid the most troubling aspects of discipline and examination. The educator may need to make transparent the strategies of power in the classroom and implicate himself or herself in those strategies. Furthermore, as I ask students to introduce their identities, the exercise is limited insomuch as I am helping them to make a correction to their consciousness. As discussed in chapter 3, work on consciousness is best left to the student. At the least, I need to reflect on my purpose and intent as an educator, since the exercise is akin to sorting and differentiating individuals from each other. Upon reflection about the limits of my earlier approach to identity claims, I now emphasize the importance of speaking to identity as a discursive practice. That is, I am less veiled in my request and ask students to consider how speaking to social location through discourse affects the social reality of the classroom. In this way, the speaking of identity is not so much an exercise of exposing the "authentic self" or separating out the parts of self that are most important. Rather, students can use the identity claim as a political act to reshape the discursive environment as a whole rather than simply revealing their personal consciousness of identity.

Rather than students thinking they are offering the core of their identities or an authentic expression of their identities for the professor to correct through an improved consciousness, I hope that we all become reflective about how we reveal ourselves to coconstruct the discursive terrain together. By making present the modalities of the self, such as discourse and language, power relationships, and expressions of the self, each of us considers how the classroom is socially constructed and how it acts as a laboratory for considering how we might change troubling social relations.

Furthermore, the claim to identity needs to be reconsidered in light of the fact that the classroom is no longer contained within the boundaries of four walls in a space away from other influences. With the move to online teaching and the increasing use of commercial technologies and video for teaching, the broader influences of capitalism and neoliberalism are clearly present in the classroom (K. Smith, 2007). The idea of an insular self that can be reflected on in a safe classroom separate from broader influences no longer holds.

The Ongoing Influence of the Enlightenment on Expression of the Self

The exercise of identity claims just discussed is troubling in another aspect, since it invites students to think of identity as unitary and coherent. In addition, it could be argued that I am asking them to unify their identities based on an exaggerated emphasis on those aspects that are tied most to their marginalization (Moffatt, 2006). The Enlightenment approach to social work education dies hard as I continue to treat each student as a unitary self that can develop an improved consciousness through my intervention (Irving, 1994, 1999, 2014). This approach to teaching encourages the students to imagine a unitary self that can induce a reflective process that works counter to social awareness and change.

The risk is that by calling out for identity claims, I am encouraging students to make their personal consciousness the center of historical development rather than helping them to be open to diversity and difference. As Foucault explains,

If the history of thought could remain the locus of uninterrupted continuities, if it could endlessly forge connexions that no analysis could undo without abstraction, if it could weave, around everything that men say and do, obscure synthesis that anticipate for him, prepare him, and lead him endlessly towards his future, it would provide a privileged shelter for the sovereignty of consciousness. Continuous history is the indispensable correlative

of the founding function of the subject: the guarantee that everything that has eluded him may be restored to him; the certainty
that time will disperse nothing without restoring it in a reconstituted unity; the promise that one day the subject—in the form
of historical consciousness—will once again be able to appropriate, to bring back under his sway, all those things that are kept at
a distance by difference, and find in them what might be called
his abode. Making historical analysis the discourse of the continuous and making human consciousness the original subject of
all historical development and all action are the two sides of the
same system of thought. In this system, time is conceived in terms
of totalization and revolutions are never more than moments of
consciousness. (1972, 12)

Foucault states that solely making one aware of consciousness is
a conservative form of intervention. Analysis that brings all forces
back to continuous history, as well as an improved consciousness,
does not allow for a real revolution of relationships. The dual
focus on continuous history and individual consciousness total-
izes all experience to serve the purpose of constituting the consciousness of the individual (Foucault, 1972). The danger is that
we teach to identity in a manner that becomes an exercise of
reclaiming the self while clinging to an uninterrupted consciousness. This uninterrupted consciousness is actually what I hope
my pedagogical approach can help change and reconstitute in
order to allow for personal and social change. I would add that
the exercise does not allow for reflection so deep that it leads to
the reconstitution of the psyche and social relationships discussed
in the previous chapter. Also, it does not allow for the disruption of the concept of the self that may be necessary for social
change, which I discuss in the conclusion. Furthermore, the

awareness necessary for social change requires a break from the discursive claims, such as new managerialism and the technological worldview, that already promote individualism and distance in relationship.

Even while I am concerned about students declaring their identities, the classroom in large, urban, public, postsecondary educational institutions has become a site of struggle in terms of dealing with issues of diversity. The educational challenges become complex in social work classes in which the course content must deal not only with the social context of the classroom but also with the social dynamics within the class itself. An awareness develops among the students and the professor of how the classroom can act as a microcosm of broader social realities (Yee and Wagner, 2013).

I have noticed, upon reflection, that at times I treat the classroom dynamics as if they were a simple replication of broader social relationships. The ideas of a constraining network of social relationships, the value of individual identity, and the need to change consciousness are highly valued in progressive politics and teaching. This type of analysis is increasingly unsatisfactory for me, since the classroom is permeable to a constant, shifting, and real-time array of influences. I believe these concepts—constraining social relationships, the value of individual identity, and the need for a change of consciousness—continue to be helpful but do not do justice to the constant, surprising interplay of dynamics arising from technological incursions, as well as from the radical diversity in the contemporary classroom. This type of analysis is limited insomuch as macro social relationships are imagined as a box or a constraining structure, with each identity conceptualized as insular. Furthermore, this analysis may lead to the belief that social consciousness is an uninterrupted consciousness that only needs to be slightly corrected rather than reconstituted. The faulty logic is that if one reflects solely on oneself, then one contributes to the personal well-being of all and to the progressive march of history through improved consciousness.

In summary, it is possible that the focus on personal identity could contribute to a conservative approach to social relations wherein the identity is imagined as insular, afloat on the precarious sea of troubling relationships outlined in chapter 1. I now enrich Foucault's understanding of power and knowledge with Deleuze and Guattari's (1987) concepts of the planar, assemblage, and rhizomatic change.

DELEUZE AND GUATTARI

Deleuze was a philosopher who had published a large body of work before meeting Guattari in 1969. He was a creative philosopher who taught at Vincennes University outside Paris. Guattari was the director of the La Borde psychiatric clinic in France, a radical psychoanalyst, a social scientist, and the author of many articles. He was involved in political militancy in France (Dosse, 2010).

When the two men met in 1969, they developed a working relationship and published two groundbreaking books, *Anti-Oedipus* and *A Thousand Plateaus* (Dosse, 2010). Deleuze and Guattari's (1987) seminal text *A Thousand Plateaus* consists of a series of concepts set out in a nonlinear and nonprogressive manner. The concepts are not necessarily introduced to support an overall argument. Instead, the authors encourage the reader to read the book from any point rather than from beginning to end.

In the introduction to the book, Deleuze and Guattari argue that the book is neither a subject nor an object but rather an assemblage, since it is made of various formed matters.

According to Deleuze and Guattari (1987), philosophers too often have acted as domesticated servants of the state. They outlined the principles of philosophy that supported relationships of dominance in hopes of challenging those relationships and rethinking the purpose of philosophy. According to Jorgensen and Yob (2013), the system of thought that Deleuze and Guattari hoped to overturn includes the following elements:

- The logic of working from tenets of abstract reason that are presented as neutral and nonemotional in nature
- The avoidance of, and separating out of, minority interests in order to suppress that thought
- The assumption that the main trajectory of thought is defined by the thinking of white males
- Closed systems of thought that are self-referential

In order to achieve an inversion of Western philosophical thought, Deleuze and Guattari (1987) utilize a number of metaphors that capture ideas about social change. Some of those metaphors are *multiplicities*, *segmentaries*, *intensities*, *lines of flights*, *the planar*, *assemblage*, and *rhizomatic change*. I outline the last three of these concepts to think about the classroom.

The Planar

Deleuze and Guattari (1987) avoid dualistic foci on change. For example, the authors avoid such binary concepts as intrapsychic versus sociological forms of change. In this manner, they also avoid the psychological search for the "deep" problem in intrapsychic issues that is separate from social affairs. Rather, they focus on the planar, which involves imagining how elements are placed beside one another and in relationship to one another. If we imagine elements as diverse as sexual orientations, technology, acts, and symbols in proximity to one another in the classroom, then we can avoid the logic that one of these modes completely defines the other elements. In this manner, we avoid a dualistic or categorical interpretation of the classroom as a whole, as well as of the students as individuals (Moffatt, 2012a). When we focus in the classroom on the elements that are beside each other, we are less likely to search for and create categorical, reductive, and scientific definitions of human affairs dictated by dualisms such as subject versus object, antecedent versus precedent, and cause versus effect (Moffatt, 2001a, 2012a).

Conceptualizing the classroom along the lines of the planar may help the educator, through reflection, to be more conscious of strategic power relationships such as discipline and examination. We may be more cautious in rushing to the "right response" to a social issue. We can avoid the faulty logic that defines the authentic expression of the self as being tied to the Enlightenment notions of the self and personal change. We do not focus reflection and change solely on the consciousness of the individual, as if it existed outside the parameters of social relationships and many other elements of the classroom.

The "spatial positionality of *beside* . . . seems to offer some useful resistance to the ease with which *beneath* and *beyond* turn from spatial descriptors into implicit narratives of, respectively, origin and telos" (Sedgwick, 2003, 8). Juxtaposing the various elements makes possible "a wide range of desiring, identifying, representing, repelling, paralleling, differentiating, rivalling, learning, twisting, mimicking, withdrawing, attracting, aggressing, warping, and other relations" (Sedgwick, 2003, 8). Space in the classroom therefore takes on a rich dimension (Sedgwick, 2003) from the philosophical, artistic, social, and moral points of view. The ephemeral quality of the space further enriches the experience of the planar (*beside*) rather than the historical origins of the event (*before*) or the psychology of the participants (*beneath*) (Moffatt, 2012a). The shift from dichotomous thought opens the possibility of multiplicity in subjectivities and expressions of agency (Irving and Moffatt, 2002; Irving and Young, 2002).

Assemblage

There is a tendency among academics to imagine the classroom as an entity with a linear process based on a taken-for-granted unitary developmental movement that goes through stages leading to resolution. This frame for thinking is evident in the construction of classroom objectives and measurable outcomes for the course. When the classroom is imagined as a unitary entity with a forward movement toward a more progressive reality, most reflective change seems to become the responsibility of the students. Students are expected to change themselves at the core of their being in order to reflect the forward movement of the educator's teaching.

Based on the thought of Deleuze and Guattari, Youdell and McGimpsey (2015) invite us to analyze the classroom in order to understand both its disassembly and its reassembly rather than imagining it as unitary whole. When one imagines the classroom as *assemblage*, reflective analysis becomes a way to think about how the diverse elements combine to create productive relationships. Rather than focus on the solitary and individualized identities of people, we think about the combination and relationship of elements across relationships (Deleuze and Guattari, 1987). The focus then becomes the multiple meanings, significances, realizations, and potentialities as they are tied to movements, flows, and productive relationships in the classroom. No element of the classroom is "background noise," nor is any element of the classroom banal and inconsequential.

Rather than thinking of the classroom as a series of competing identities based on the social location of each student, I now attempt to think of it as a form of assemblage. The assemblage is both trans-scalar and multiorder (Deleuze and Guattari, 1987; Youdell and McGimpsey, 2015). Rather than containing levels of social order that need to be viewed in a different light from each other, such as policy versus practice, the assemblage is made up of elements across scales (Deleuze and Guattari, 1987). The educational institution can be understood as an assemblage that is made up of heterogeneous components that cut across discursive, state, institutional, economic, social, and subjective orders. Youdell and McGimpsey invite us to imagine that the assemblage "might include economy, monetary flows, state, legislation, policy, institutions, organizations, social and cultural forms, discourse, representation, subjectivities and affectivities" (2015, 119). The assemblage in the classroom also is created from components as wide ranging as institutional influences, politics, policy, economics, affect, subjectivity, media, and everyday practices (Deleuze and Guattari, 1987; Youdell and Armstrong, 2011). Assemblage includes common taken-for-granted elements of the course, such as the course outline, the web-based software for course management, and the grading system. So too, personal subjectivities are in the mix of classroom elements and become relevant to education when the classroom is imagined as an assemblage. The influences and elements can be so precise and diverse as to include the commercials we inadvertently play on YouTube when we are about to show an educational video. When we imagine the classroom as an assemblage, we reflect on all elements of the classroom, whether technical or human.

Rather than being future oriented, staged, and linear, time can be imagined in differing ways in the classroom as well. Each component is introduced into the classroom at a different time, such as the lecture that I have reworked from a previous session, the article that was written a few years before it was introduced into the curriculum, and my age as I enter the classroom each year. The differing effects of these components are influenced by this dating of materials and relationships. So too, articulation and expression in the classroom have differing speeds (Deleuze and Guattari, 1987). This has been a very useful concept for me, since I seldom react within the moment but rather reflect over time about the classroom experience.

Social entities created through assemblage can be imagined as a whole, but they are always transitory and mobile. By drawing on this concept of assemblage, I can better imagine the ebb and flow of relations in my classroom. According to Deleuze and Guattari (1987), the assemblage is made up of lines of flight, of movement, and of articulation. The subjectivities of students present in the classroom represent multiscalar realities. These subjectivities or subjects in process are present in a manner that can disrupt taken-for-granted discourse. Certain policies or discourses, such as neoliberalism and new managerialism, influence the classroom as a whole, but also can vary in their intensity from time to time. At times, these influences are elusive, fragmentary, and incomplete.

At the same time, all subjectivities may be influenced by institutional preference. For example, the preferred conceptualization of the neoliberal student is as a self-starting entrepreneur (Moffatt et al., 2016; Pollack and Rossiter, 2010). This preferred subjectivity of the student is common and highly valued in the university where I teach and, in this way, becomes one of the multiscalar influences on the classroom experience. Students take on the institutional expectations of the entrepreneur, imagine what the discourse means, and express themselves accordingly. This expression might occur even when such subjectivity is not being discussed in the classroom or, in fact, is being openly critiqued. At other times, the expression of the entrepreneur may be distorted or fragmented depending on how other components combine in the classroom to allow for subjective engagement by students.

Rhizomatic Change

Imagining the classroom as planar and constructed through assemblage leads us to question the approach to knowledge that seeks to better understand the deeper or underlying significance of social relationships. Most philosophical Western thought is based on the metaphor of the tree with deep roots. The taproot approach to education is based on the idea that thought prospers and grows from the depths of the root (Dosse, 2010). Through the taproot approach to knowledge, we try to understand what is foundational to thought and what lies under the surface of what we know. Whatever is at the root of thought is what helps to build the rest of the approach to education. The taproot approach to knowledge invites us to conceptualize thought as if it were hierarchical, objective, closed, static, and abstract (Deleuze and Guattari, 1987).

This approach to meaning making creates the necessity to find deeper significance than that to which we are exposed. One is constantly seeking the transcendent that exists outside the social influence on thought (Jorgensen and Yob, 2013). A danger of the taproot approach to knowledge is that it encourages us to ignore all the components of the classroom or reconceptualize them as insignificant. As previously mentioned, it can constitute reflective thinking as a conservative process as it becomes a form of thinking that encourages students to reflect on and only consider the transcendent or "deeper" influences. An example of this type of thinking is when students are encouraged to reach into the depths of their souls to be better prepared to aid in social change. Another example might be the belief that students can reconstitute the psyche as if it existed outside all the classroom components and broader troubling social relationships.

In contrast to the taproot approach to knowledge, Deleuze and Guattari (1987) argue for a *rhizomatic change* based on the metaphor of the rhizome root. A rhizome is a subterranean stem that is different from deep roots. It assumes a variety of diverse forms, from surface extension in all directions to the concentration of the root into bulbs and tubers. In terms of knowledge, the rhizome is nonhierarchical and exists without a central focal point or one overall organizing principle. According to Deleuze and Guattari, "Unlike trees or their roots, the rhizome connects any point to any other point, and its traits are not necessarily linked to traits of the same nature; it brings into play very different regimes of signs and even non-sign states. The rhizome is reducible neither to the One nor to the multiple" (1987, 21).

As a metaphor for knowledge, the rhizome does not have one primary or foundational conceptual form. Since there is not an underlying concept that links all knowledge, the development of concepts is open to change and is influenced by the flow of ideas among component parts of the classroom. The rhizome does not seek a pure form that is untarnished; rather, it includes both the best and the worst of relations (Deleuze and Guattari, 1987). The rhizomatic is an inversion of the classical Western approach to philosophy, since "this objectified, striated, hierarchical, transcendent, logical, closed, static, abstract realm of thought is now to be repudiated in favor of its inversion—a subjectified, politicized, mystical, cosmic, flat, imminent, smooth, open, dynamic, abstract realm of thought" (Jorgensen and Yob, 2013, 38).

Rather than seeking the true meaning or the deeper meaning of a person, substance, or thought, the rhizomatic approach to meaning can be chaotic and amorphous. Rhizomatic thought can respond to differing conditions and can grow in a number of directions. It is not constrained by the foundational concept of authentic or true meaning that must be delved into to be understood (Jorgensen and Yob, 2013). When the rules and regulations for proper inquiry are opened up, new approaches to knowledge can flourish. We are freed of the self-referential unitary thinking that Foucault cautions against in the passage quoted earlier, whereby reflection becomes an exercise too easily focused on examination and discipline. It also becomes a process of capturing thinking through, and reflecting on surprising and new approaches to knowledge (Irving and Moffatt, 2002; Irving and Young, 2002).

The classroom as rhizome might be imagined as a map that is reversible and modifiable and has many entries and exits. All things in the rhizome are in the *manner of becomings*. The rhizome "operates by variation, expansion, conquest, capture, off-shoots" (Deleuze and Guattari, 1987, 21). Rather than having a beginning or end, the rhizome involves a variety of dimensions and directions in motion. In other words, it is made up of a number of linear multiplicities. The assemblage of the classroom is defined by circulation linked to all things, including politics, technology, animal and vegetal elements, politics, the economy, sexuality, and desire (Deleuze and Guattari, 1987). Rhizomatic change considers these diverse elements and the many eccentric ways in which they can be combined to create meaning. Reflection becomes complex in the case of rhizomatic change since it is about making sense of a plethora of elements. Those elements include our emotions, affects, and technologies of teaching in the context of complex diversities and subjectivities.

REFLECTION: ATTEMPTING RHIZOMATIC CHANGE IN A QUEER THEORIES CLASS

I have attempted to make the concepts of assemblage and rhizomatic change more palpable and present in a Queer Theories and Identities course that I teach at the undergraduate level. The course objectives include the following:

- To develop an understanding of the historical, social, geopolitical, and economic relations of power through which queer and otherwise sexed or gendered lives are lived

- To become familiar with current knowledge and debates circulating within lesbian, gay, bisexual, trans, and all queer communities
- To develop familiarity with key concepts related to queer theory and their application to specific sites of ethical consideration and social work practice

In the past, I have taught the Queer Theories course as if I have been the holder of a "superior" knowledge about the many forms of gender and sexuality. Furthermore, I have assumed that prejudice and social ignorance exist among certain students about alternative gender and sexual expression. This professorial posture of enlightened or superior knowledge is difficult to give up as a professor. In the past I have had to correct in myself, through reflection, a similar posture in a graduate social work class at Smith College. In that case, I realized that I did not have a better understanding of the concept of shame than my students. I realized that I had begun the class by assuming I had to convince the classroom about shame, but through the classroom experience I realized that I had much to learn about shame from the female students because of my gendered experience as a male (Moffatt, 2004).

In an ongoing attempt to work against my own tendency to take a teaching posture that refers to rarified concepts that lie outside the influence of classroom components, I have explored the framework formulated by Deleuze and Guattari that I just outlined. Presently, I attempt to attend to assemblage and how it influences my teaching. I also attempt to make the many elements of assemblage visible in the classroom by speaking about them. By discussing these elements, as well as the relationship between them, I hope to encourage reflective awareness of them.

Students and I can reflect both cognitively and emotionally on these elements.

In order to make more obvious the components of assemblage, I have introduced a student presentation element in a class the Queer Theories class. Students are invited to choose the topic for presentation as long as they can convincingly argue that it is focused on queer studies. Presentations can include social analysis, personal stories, media critique, and works of art. Students also are able to choose the mode and content of analysis so that the method of engagement with their colleagues is open ended. In this course, students have presented poetry, original music, book reviews, media analysis, cultural studies, and autobiography in their presentations. The students also use a wide variety of technologies, such as video clips, sound files, images, and musical instruments. It is my contention that the variety of presentation methods, along with the use of many technologies, makes assemblage more obvious in the classroom and can allow for rhizomatic change.

Although presentation is a common teaching modality, it is my hope that the purpose and the methods of the presentation create a differing awareness for the students. This exercise is based in part on a voice of gay liberation, which is a component of the assemblage in its own right. That is, it has been my hope that everyone in the classroom finds a voice and is given the opportunity to express their subjectivity (Moffatt, 2012a). Now, through the student presentation, I hope to allow for some form of rhizomatic change in the classroom. I am open to the flux of each cohort of students having its own character and eccentricities. It is my role as the educator to make sense, through reflection with the students, of our experience together and at times make transparent the components of assemblage so that we can reflect together on them. I am also now aware that the expression of the students' voices and their messages is influenced by the rhizomatic change that occurs within the classroom.

The variety of topics and methods students choose for their presentations is tied to the singular creative voice of each student in a manner that I hope makes all classroom participants develop a beginning awareness of the multiple subjects in process in the classroom (see the discussion of Julia Kristeva in chapter 3). I also hope that the exercise makes obvious more components tied to assemblage and rhizomatic change, including the method of technology the students use to present and the tone with which they choose to express themselves. For myself, some of the more affecting technologies have been acoustic guitar, voice, handwritten posters, and zines. When I introduce this exercise, I hope that the diversity within the classroom takes on its own life rather than accentuating competitiveness and individualism. Furthermore, this exercise continues to offer the opportunity to disrupt taken-for-granted discursive frames about identity, such as student as entrepreneur or consumer, that also contribute to the tone of the classroom (Todd et al., 2017).

In addition to this presentation, I encourage students to talk freely about topics in the class, even if those topics seem tangentially related to course content. In this manner, I encourage associational thinking that might be better suited to understanding the planar. I have learned through this teaching method that it is impossible to address from the lecture podium the multiple concerns and interests of the students. Even as a professor who values cultural studies and believes in the importance of understanding the influence of pop culture, I am taken aback by students' interests. I was fascinated by the presentation of an Asian woman who did an in-depth analysis of a superhero character and talked openly about sexual acts and gender disidentification in Marvel products. I was surprised at the wide-ranging discussion among students about a Disney movie that ended up engaging a wide variety of racialized students in a complex discussion about the processes of racialization. I was shocked at how many students of all races, genders, and sexualities watch instructional makeup videos on YouTube and have a political interpretation of those videos.

The assemblage includes the diversity of people, the diversity of subjects in process, the diversity of topics, and the diversity of methods for content delivery. Furthermore, it includes the technological influences from outside the classroom, such as social media and commercial imagery, that contribute to students' experiences of their selves. Each student experiences his or her own assemblage. I believe, for example, that the wide-ranging discussion of Disney was a form of rhizomatic change. I could not have so successfully engaged the students in my class without letting the discussion flow and refraining from insisting that they choose a "proper" source of information.

The loose nature of the assignment means each of us in the classroom is exposed to unresolved ideas, fractured realities, and sound bites of thought. In fact, it might be argued that the neoliberal focus of the university, discussed in chapter 1, and the consumerist culture that is the context for education, discussed in chapter 3, increase this sense of fragmentation because of the increasing tolerance of short time frames for thought and practice and the quick resolution of ideas. This exposure to the rapid development of ideas or the flash of an incomplete thought or fractured symbol is not unlike daily experience in the media-saturated, technology-driven environment within which we exist.

These fragmentary ideas or expressions are part of the rhizomatic change in a classroom defined by the planar.

By encouraging the expression of queer subjectivities in the classroom through presentation, we can reflect on the experience of multiplicity in relationships. Students and educators can also reflect on ascesis and experience each other's subjectivities, or how we make ourselves present in the space. We can also experience and reflect on how the revealing of the self teaches us the frustrations and limitations of representation while allowing us to experience the liberating quality of being present in diversity (Moffatt, 2012a). At best, the presentations create a form of cacophony (Irving and Young, 2002; Irving and Moffatt, 2002; E. Keenan, Miehls, Moffatt, Orwat, and White, 2004) that is very much in line with rhizomatic change in the assemblage.

At the same time, each component in the classroom—in particular, the subjective engagement of students—relates to the organism but also can disrupt by breaking through to dismantle our intentions and our experience (Butler 2006c; Deleuze and Guattari, 1987). There are many disclosures in this class, such as that of the white, straight-identified student who cried because her gay uncle was in a custody dispute with the birth mother of his adoptive son; that of the straight, black, female student who is the sole person to carry the secret of her father's gay identity; and that of the questioning white, cisgender male student with a suicidal gay brother. Furthermore, expressions of subjectivity that have taken me by surprise include how students negotiate gender and sexuality through fanzines and online gamer communities. The concept of a whole and pure identity and the categorization of identity through binary thinking—in this case, my tendency to think of identity as either straight or gay and focused on either gender or sexuality—dissipate through this sharing. The Queer Theory and Identities classroom becomes a place of multiplicities.

I have learned much about identification and associations about the self through a looser approach to expression in the classroom (Hyatt, 2014; Hyatt and Good, 2017). I learned that what music one listens to is an important identifier for the students today, just as it was when I was an adolescent. I have learned about the surprising resilience of and interest in punk rock among young students, even so many years after it was introduced as an art form. I learned that the "questioning" category of identity formation is key for students today who want to talk about sexual and gender identity but remain uncertain of their own. I have learned how identity construction and personal disclosures are tied to relationships with others, as discussed in chapters 2 and 3. I believe that a differing manifestation of assemblage according to participants, timing, and trans-scalar influences will lead to differing lessons with each manifestation of the classroom, and my lessons are likely to be different with each iteration.

At times, emotional or affective responses including anxiety, excitement, and tension emerge when the students engage as subjects in process in the class while exploring tangential interests in an associational manner. I have learned from student narratives in a way that has been emotional for me. Sometimes the subjective attachment of students to a topic and their ability to express it have been remarkably affecting. At times, these emotions have been surprising to me. Topics and stories bring to the fore deeply held emotive responses, and these responses are part of rhizomatic change. For example, the student who had a self-harming queer family member and was questioning her own sexual orientation told me she can talk about suicide and contain her emotional responses as long as there are no images of blood in the classroom presentations.

REFLECTION: THE LIMITS AND POSSIBILITIES OF DELEUZE AND GUATTARI

Still, there are problems with the approach of rhizomatic change, which is dependent on students expressing the self as a subject in process in the classroom. The shift to components of the class-room that increase the number of possibilities for expression can make some identity expressions outliers. For example, some trans people feel their gender both precedes and persists in spite of socialization so that they "have always felt [their] gender, thus, transition makes it possible to become the person one always knew one was" (Pyne, 2016, 62). A foundational claim to the nature of one's gender, which is important to the safety and self-worth of some trans people, seems to be in contradiction to the fluidity and partial expressions being imagined by the professor who promotes change through partial discoveries, attachment to multiple components of the classroom, and associational think-ing. In this way, the trans voice may once again be problema-tized and mistreated as the outlier to progressive social change (Pyne, 2016).

It is nearly impossible to imagine students engaging in asce-sis and becoming subjects in process as class sizes creep up in the new managerialist university. For example, in the Queer Theories class, there are twelve weeks to engage thirty-eight students in presentations, lectures, course management, consul-tation, and discussion. The brief time that can be allotted to a student presentation is tied to increasing class sizes. One has to be extremely efficient in time allocation, and this makes present in the assemblage of the classroom the component of efficiency, which is a product of neoliberal ideology and the technical approach to education. The creation of space for student presentations becomes increasingly difficult in the context of the neoliberal contemporary classroom. The small amount of time available for presentations is a manifestation of the broader social relations that constitute larger classrooms, forcing professors to expect truncated and sporadic student participation. Furthermore, the many risks students take in terms of expressing themselves in the classroom might become disconcerting and confusing in the context of an institution that values technique, credentialism, and technological learning.

There are constraints to imagining the classroom as an assemblage, such as the way students are individualized during presentations and the manner in which I sit in judgment and examination as I watch them present. While the students present, I take notes to help me remember who they are and to stay engaged in what interests each of them. This is the first step in the process of examination and discipline described earlier. The process continues through a logic of signifiers that eventually leads to the reductive exercise of grading the students (Moffatt, 2006). This form of judgment and categorization is yet another element of assemblage, so we need to be attentive to how it disrupts the associational interactions and learning in the class.

The rocky path of introducing student presentations has caused me to engage in reflection based in self-doubt as an educator. Was I simply replicating my power by demanding a frenzied schedule? Did the tight schedule of presentations contribute to a lack of depth of analysis? Was I encouraging students to act as neoliberal subjects focused on their individualism? By moving to the concept of assemblage, how was I distorting claims to identities, such as gay, lesbian, bi, queer, trans, and two spirited, that are highly valued as political subjectivities by some students in the class?

In spite of these difficulties, I continue to insist that each student present to the class. I no longer insist, however, that students make their identities the focus of the presentation or the starting point of engagement in my class. I hope, however, the drive for attachment, can be expressed, though I still remind myself that "what a human being can articulate of that (somatic) self" is a question "that must remain open" (Pyne, 2016, 68).

Upon reading Deleuze and Guattari, I believe I underwent a shift in my role as reflective educator. In the past, my teaching was mostly concerned with signifiers and language and how they are made present in the classroom through identity claims. I now believe that an additional role of the educator is to help map or survey the classroom for the many components of assemblage. This type of mapping, done with the students, can take note of more elusive phenomena such as attachments that evolve among students, the intensity of engagement of participants in the classroom, and ruptures in experience, whether through technological incursions or the welcome disruption of surprising voices. Some of these I comment on, and others I note for my own reflection but do not feel that they need to be pointed out. As educators, we can reflect on a micropolitics of relationships between components of the classroom, so we move with the shifts within the classroom rather than stay focused on our prior expectations. Space, such as classroom space, is not seen as inert or neutral. Rather, it is geo-ontological in that it is an aggregate of distinctive yet connective relationships with differing flows, resonances, and intensities between them. Classroom space based on the concept of the rhizome is generative, and the relationship between elements is as significant as the elements themselves (Roy, 2005).

DISCUSSION

In this chapter, I have reflected on how, by asking students to make identity claims, I have often been engaged in the power strategies of discipline and examination. I currently strive to engage in reflection that is based on the linked concepts of the classroom as planar and as an assemblage, with a focus on rhizomatic change. The introduction of the student presentation, although an old pedagogical method, has a new purpose in this case. I hope to make present and map with the students the assemblage, including components such as the multiplicity of expressions in the class, their diverse cultural and social influences, and the technologies of education. We can map and reflect on influences beyond our interpersonal exchanges in the classroom. I have come to understand components of the classroom that I thought of as noise in the past, such as the discussion of pop culture or the intrusion of computers, to be part of the assemblage and therefore part of the politics of the classroom worthy of reflection. Most importantly, I continue to strive to make present the multiplicities of student voice.

Reflection continues to serve the necessary purposes I had thought through in the past. As I have argued in the past, we reflect on our practice in order to protect against dangerous practices and troubling knowledge development. So too, we reflect in order to correct for prejudicial knowledge of the other. In an acknowledgment of the many diversities and the wide array of components present within the classroom, reflection by students and educators takes on an enriched meaning. Reflection is not only self-critical; it also allows students the opportunity to reconsider the specificity and the context of each other's life histories (Witkin, 2014a) and to think about how ascesis feels and changes through social interactions. Reflection is further enriched when we examine the discursive construction of each of our selves in the context of a multiplicity of influences (Chambon and Irving, 2003; Irving, 1999). Reflection, in the context of assemblage, becomes focused on the many eccentric ways that components combine in the classroom.

The principle of multiple possible methods for change within the context of diverse attachments and connections in the classroom can be confusing. With many people attempting to create symbols tied to affect, as discussed in chapter 3, one can feel emotionally and cognitively overwhelmed. These responses can lead one to feel a sense of vulnerability and precariousness. The individual voices of students become tentative, veiled, or fully expressed depending on the interplay of the components of assemblage. For example, the young students I teach increasingly self-define as questioning or queer. I think this identification is positive and productive, since the students are taking risks while being aware that the self is open ended and constantly reflective.

I am deeply attached to the topic of queer theories and identity, since I socially identify as a gay man. This attachment has created a subjectivity for me that is emotionally engaged. At times I am blinded to new queer possibilities as I try to stand firm in my emotional response. At times, I am "keeping myself together" so as not to cry in public either for my own hurts or as an empathetic response to a student's story (Doyle, 2013). Such is the feeling of precariousness. In order to stay in role of educator, I may choose to stand in emotional and cognitive isolation—the final refuge for the professor careering out of control. But rhizomatic change allows one to reflect on "multiple entrances organized by unknown laws and principles of distribution. . . . We will therefore enter at any point" (Deleuze and Guattari cited in Dosse, 2010, 241). My own reactions are important, but they are part of a wide range of multiplicities in the classroom and only one point of intervention. No wonder I retreat to my office and close the door after teaching such classes.

5

THE DISPOSSESSED SELF

In chapter 2, I argued that one of the strengths of reflective practice in social work is the focus on the self. Rather than treat reflective practice as an adjustment of method or a technical change in the direction of method, the social worker is called on to reflect on the socially constituted self. In chapter 3, I discussed student consciousness and the need for a psychic space in which students can reflect on both the psyche and social relations. In chapter 4, I pushed the boundaries of the self by considering the many components, both human and technical, of the classroom space that affect subjective engagement. In this chapter I turn my attention to the reflective educator. By exploring the presence of the educator in the social work classroom, I argue that we become aware of our influence in the classroom, as well as the value of imagining the self as changeable. I begin by discussing the educator as a reflexive self who is socially constituted. Then, building on the concept of the reflexive self, I advocate for the idea of dispossessed educator who is open to vulnerability and a feeling of dispossession to the point of *coming undone*. I begin the discussion of the professor's role and identity by focusing on masculinity and race.

PATTERNS OF DOMINANCE

The educator's role is constructed through social relations and expectations, but at the same time, the presence of the professor affects those interpersonal relationships that define the classroom (see, for example, Moffatt, 2001b, 2004; Sirotich et al., 2012) As discussed in the previous chapter, the educator's presence is a matrix of power and knowledge whereby subjectivity is constructed through the flux of power and its contingent knowledge creation (Fook, 2016).

The presence of the professor is supported by subjective truth claims (Youdell and Armstrong, 2011). Truth is not an essence to be discovered but instead lies within the play of social relations between people (Chambon, 1999; Foucault, 1980a; Irving, 1999). The many combinations of power and knowledge invite a multiplicity of truths. The microanalysis of specific relations leads us to understand how knowledge of our own and others' identities is constructed (Foucault 1980a, 1980c, 1988b). With this play of relationships, it follows that because of the multiple links of power and knowledge in the classroom, the professor has many identities (Pease, 1999), each tied to the many ways the students and professor construct knowledge about each other (Todd, 2012). In this manner, markers of identity such as race, class, and gender come into play in the classroom (Yee and Wagner, 2013).

Masculinity

At the same time, identity is not a simple cause and effect of social interaction but is rather rewarded or made invisible through its congruence with broader social settings and social relations (Kristeva, 2002a; Moffatt, 2004; Pease, 1999). For example, since gendered and racialized networks of masculine power are so entrenched and omnipresent, if I do not reflect on my masculinity and whiteness, I am likely to support gendered and racialized patterns of dominance (Heron, 2005; Moffatt, 2012b). One subjective truth claim assumes that the masculine subject is tied to social relations that are rational, objective, and neutral (Moffatt, 2012c). This type of claim has a dual purpose of supporting neoliberal and new managerial structures of power, on one hand, and entrenching the social power of the male, on the other hand. Another such matrix of knowledge and power emerges when masculinity is tied to the assumption that social relations are commonsensical, no matter how inequitable those relationships. Common sense becomes a social concept that supports male strategies of power. As long as men do not interrogate personal identity as a social construction, they do not have to reflect on the troubling social relations tied to masculinity (Moffatt, 2004; Pease, 1999). It follows that as long as maleness is not made the object of reflection, the ways that male power contributes to the mistreatment, exclusion, and marginalization of others go unchecked (see Moffatt, 2004, 2012b, 2012c).

At the same time that the masculine subject is taken for granted or assumed to be common sense, a social bias exists based on the assumption that the act of creating symbolic language is the preserve of the male (Kristeva, 1982; Moffatt, 2004). Even though the university is strongly associated with creating symbols and knowledge, the manner in which symbolic language is tied to the strategies of masculine power is rendered invisible (Kristeva, 1982; Baileyegu et al., 2000). So too, the concept of a single type of masculinity renders the masculine unactionable and unchangeable. Through the practice of deconstruction, the multiplicity in masculinity can be revealed and a reconstruction and rethinking of multiple masculinities is possible. This might create a new agency for the male subject, especially the male who has experienced marginalization based on race, sexuality, gender expression, class, or ability, so that he can imagine new discourses of masculinity (Moffatt, 2012c; Pease, 1999, Sirotich et al., 2012). Specifically, I argue that the politics of performativity contributes to the constitution of the professor's experience and presence in the classroom.

Performativity

According to Butler (1997), gender is socially constructed through performative acts. A series of discursive practices are enacted that both restrict and bind gender expression. These discursive practices tend to create binaries that define how it is possible to be a man or a woman. While some performances of gender may be voluntary acts, *performativity* refers to those acts that are compulsory and reinforced through both micropractices and institutional practices. The practices become effective through repetition over time. These repetitive discursive practices also create exclusions through the construction of gendered expectations (Butler, 1997; Moffatt, 2004). As a professor, I engage in a series of acts and discursive practices that constitute not only me as a male but also the genders of the students in the class.

By standing in front of a classroom, the male professor is engaging in a performative act, especially in the case of the social work classroom, which predominantly contains female students.

My standing posture at the front of a group of seated women creates gender possibilities and limitations. When information or knowledge is disseminated through lecture rather than dialogue, one is involved in a performative act that conveys that the male professor knows about and is expert in symbol creation. Furthermore, when I introduce the symbols and language in the lecture notes through a commercial vehicle of knowledge dissemination such as PowerPoint, I further reinforce the concept that symbol creation is the preserve of the male. The force of these acts lies in the weekly repetition of them. Through them, I reinforce my "solidity" as a male gendered person (Butler, 1997).

Male dominance is a strategy of social power tied to knowledge (Pease, 1999). Silence and denial can be performative acts in their own right. Male educators avoid social risk by not making present their male identities for consideration and reflection. I need to reflect on how my approach to teaching combines power and knowledge in order to elaborate strategic positions that enhance my feelings of security and power. As the regulator of the social sphere of symbolic creation, I minimize my own social risk through a certain reserve and, at times, the use of silence (Sirotich et al., 2012). In the context of this dominance, denial and avoidance are strategies to enhance a sense of personal security for men that consciously or inadvertently contributes to patterns of male dominance (Moffatt, 2004; Moffatt and Miehls, 1999).

Performative acts of gender have also created a tendency for me to think in another type of binary that creates a distinction between me and students. There are times when I take a public political or conceptual stand with students that creates an imagined separation between them and me. It is as if the students

151

and I are on different sides of a social problem because I am more enlightened. The logic is that since the students do not have "full consciousness" or do not share my point of view, their conceptualization of the social problem needs to be troubled so that they can reflect on it. I have come to understand that this personal posturing has a great deal to do with gender and is especially problematic when I am the only cisgendered male in the classroom. Through this performative act, I separate myself as the person who carries the symbols. I also separate myself as the "enlightened" professor who has a more fully developed consciousness of social affairs (Moffatt, 2004). The male strategies of being silent, on the one hand, and claiming expertise in symbol creation, on the other, are power strategies that aid me in avoiding discomfort. I avoid discomfort by evading the question of my culpability in broader troubling social relationships (Heron, 2005; Moffatt, 2004; Pon et al., 2011).

Whiteness

Similarly, white people who refuse to interrogate their influence and social presence as defined through race relations make invisible the micro and macro relations that keep unequal race relations in place (Wagner and Yee, 2011; Yee and Dumbrill, 2003). Wagner and Yee (2011) argue that this type of racial dynamic does not occur only at the level of interpersonal relations but exists throughout the overall structure of the neoliberal university. The professor who does not take a reflective approach to his or her subjectivity according to gender and race contributes to processes that treat power and knowledge as universal and beyond change (Doyle, 2013).

Pon et al. (2011) discuss how the *exalted subject* has become a complex and authoritative social work discourse based on race. The posture of the exalted subject presumes that white people are preferred and have the most to offer in helping relationships. The current overrepresentation of Aboriginal and Black children within the Canadian child welfare system is an example of the legacy of the exalted subject. The type of roles discussed in chapter 1, such as those of the friendly visitor, the voluntary service provider, and the so-called neutral professional, combined with a binary modern construction of race that separates white and racialized people, creates the discourse of the exalted subject. This discourse is tied to the modern colonial pursuit of conquering the racialized other and exploiting resources. The nonreflexive posture of a caring and kind welfare practitioner contributes to and obscures the troubling effects of the exalted subject. A reflective approach that combines critical race feminism with a postcolonial approach to understanding the social position and practices of social workers helps to deconstruct this troubling discourse. Corrective practices concerning race require a reflective approach that considers how the role of educator is tied to the construction of the nation-state, colonial relationships, the economic relations of capitalism, and the discourse of whiteness (Heron, 2005; Pon et al., 2011).

To foreclose the possibility of reflecting on aspects of myself as a white male is to retreat into the social sphere of the autonomous male. Kristeva (1982) argues that the role of men as the "rightful" members of the social realm is kept in place by thinking of the masculine as pure and the feminine as impure. Those who challenge the construction of the male gender, such as trans people, women, and queers, are socially constructed as abject in order to preserve the "pure and clean body" of the man (Kristeva,

1982). Feminine identity and those people associated with it are perceived to be threats to the individuated, pure, idealized, male body. Cisgender women, gay men, lesbians, and trans people represent the breakdown of male signifiers that have been used by men to protect the integrity of their masculinity. For some men, this also represents the breakdown of social power (Kristeva, 1982; Moffatt, 2004). In light of my subjectivity as a white male tied to power strategies associated with whiteness and masculinity (Pon et al., 2011), it is my contention that reflection is an important practice for cisgender men to work against their troubling influence (Moffatt, 2012c; Pease, 1999). In the next section, I discuss a conceptualization of the self that counters the self as a closed, nonreflexive entity.

THE REFLEXIVE SELF

The reflexive self is a mode of thinking about the self that is open to the other. In fact, the self is constituted through intersubjectivity with the other. This reflexive self allows an openness to others that enables us to rethink how we experience anxiety in relationships (Miehls and Moffatt, 2000; Moffatt and Miehls, 1999). In fact, the self can be conceptualized as a third dimension of power and knowledge (Foucault, 1988a, 1988b). In this case, reflection is tied not to changes of direction in practice but rather to the actual constitution of the self, as discussed in chapter 2 (Miehls and Moffatt, 2000). Rather than being a neutral or passive observer of relationships, the educator's self is constituted, both emotionally and cognitively, in the presence of the other: in the context of the classroom, the other is often the student (Miehls and Moffatt, 2000). The subjectivity, or the self in process, of the professor is interlinked with the subjectivity, or self in process, of the student (Miehls and Moffatt, 2000).

The Self and the Other

The ego psychology approach focuses on self-awareness through insight work. That is, when we experience anxiety in response to exposure to the other, we work to re-create the equilibrium of our self to minimize our anxious reaction. The trouble with this focus on personal consciousness that retreats to a focus on homeostasis is that the other, such as students and other educators, can become understood as the source of our anxiety (Miehls and Moffatt, 2000). In addition, as mentioned in chapter 3, this focus on regaining personal awareness and consciousness can contribute to a conservative political project.

An ego psychology approach to intrapsychic work concerning human relationships involves seeking stability. When focused solely on an intrapsychic approach, the educator may only deal with anxiety as if it were created through the external pressure that the students come to represent. In the context of a diverse classroom, the educator's feelings of instability or anxiousness might be tied to the uncertainty of dealing with a group of students of different genders, races, classes, and abilities (Miehls and Moffatt, 2000). This form of emotional management of the other by the professor is congruent with the new managerial approach to education, whereby students and professors become managers of themselves and others. The ability to respond with neutrality and reach homeostasis leading to stability is highly valued in the context of new managerialism, where subjectivities that promote management are highly valued.

If professors are preoccupied with their reactions to the other, in order to reconcile their anxiety, they may unintentionally make invisible the social diversity of students in order to achieve personal homeostasis. At the same time, discomfort for the educator may arise from discourses of diversity that are not commonly present in the classroom (Miehls and Moffatt, 2000; Moffatt, 2001b). A significant problem of the reflective approach based on the ego psychology model is that reciprocity and intersubjectivity are not adequately considered (Miehls and Moffatt, 2000).

Gilles Deleuze and Michel Foucault imagine the anxious educator as an intersubjectivity between people rather than a person who is seeking homeostasis. In this case, we can imagine that the self is not solely constituted in reaction to the other but is socially constituted alongside the other. In other words, the self is inseparably linked to social contact with the other (Miehls and Moffatt, 2000; Witkin, 2012a). As discussed in chapter 2, the self is radically social since it cannot exist outside the power and discourse of social relationships (Deleuze, 1990; Witkin, 2012a). Foucault's concepts of power come into play again, since how we view each other is determined by the nexus of knowledge, power, and practice (Fook, 2002). If this is the case, reflection on the self does the following:

- Avoids a preoccupation with our intrapsychic state in an attempt to create intrapsychic homeostasis
- Begins with the specific practices, acts, relationships, and reactions to each other within the classroom
- Is ongoing, with a focus on the many elements that create the possibility of the self, including technologies, techniques, and social relationships

- Is attentive to the multiple truths we construct about both the educator's self and the student's self (Foucault, 1980a, 1980b; Miehls and Moffatt, 2000)

Anxiety and tension, rather than being created through sources outside oneself, are actually integral to those relationships, as well as to the constitution of the self. Relationships are experienced, felt, thought through, and reflected on rather than managed (Miehls and Moffatt, 2000; Moffatt et al., 2018). In this manner the educator can work to create new possibilities for relationships with the other. The self becomes the locus of new power and knowledge strategies that, in turn, create new social possibilities. The focus is on change in relationships rather than the protection of a private psyche of determinate status (Halperin, 1995; Irving, 1999; Miehls and Moffatt, 2000). This aligns with Julia Kristeva's notion of the constantly changing self that needs to be open to continual reflection, discussed in chapter 3, and is congruent with the reflective process that deconstructs gender and race described earlier.

Social Engagement of the Reflexive Self

The reflexive self promotes a relations view of the self over the autonomous view of the self (Miehls and Moffatt, 2000; Moffatt and Miehls, 1999). The reflexive self helps us consider how we are constituted in the presence of the other. The other does not exist as an external source of discomfort but rather exists in coconstitution with our self as educator (Miehls and Moffatt, 2000). The reflexive self outlined here is congruent with the self imagined by the social work theorists discussed in chapter 2. The reflexive self also allows one to think through change in one's subjectivity in a manner that is attentive to the many elements of the classroom outlined in chapter 4. The self is integrated in a network of practices, acts, discourse, reactions to each other, and relationships (Irving, 1999; Irving, 2014). Rather than resolve anxiety, the educator pays attention to anxious reactions and reflects on the reason for anxiety (Miehls and Moffatt, 2000). Through the reflexive self, one thinks about and reflects on discomfort while being aware that discomfort need not be fully resolved. In fact, if one too quickly resolves discomfort, one may reconstruct the self as an autonomous, balanced, closed, and nonreflexive self that is not open to personal or social change, thus supporting troubling dominant discourses, or come too quickly to a decision about the self or other (Doyle, 2013; Laing, 2016).

Because of the complex social makeup of the classroom, with students' different genders, races, sexualities, classes, and abilities creating a multiplicity of social and interpersonal interactions, the educator's self also shifts and has many possible incarnations (Irving and Young, 2002; Miehls and Moffatt, 2000; Moffatt and Miehls, 1999; Pease, 1999). Although I used to worry about respectful distance in relationships, I am now cognizant of how to be aware of and present to the intersubjectivity of the students. Substitution is the exercise of putting oneself through affect and imagination in the place of the other (Miehls and Moffatt, 2000). The attempt to place oneself in the position of the other involves striving to work through affective tension while knowing that emotional resolution is ultimately unachievable (Miehls and Moffatt, 2000). So too, one can never know the experience of the other, and resolution is thus unachievable (Irving and Moffatt, 2002; Irving and Young, 2002; Kristeva,

2002c; Miehls and Moffatt, 2000). When one strives for substitution in relationships, tension and anxiety can never be resolved through a state of homeostasis of the intrapsychic self (Miehls and Moffatt, 2000).

The reflexive self outlined here alters the terms of ethical engagement in the classroom. No longer can ethical guidelines for relationships be based on principles of objectivity, confidentiality, and neutrality in order to create distance in the professional relationship. Rather, the ethics of social engagement are best defined by our obligation to the other. A number of ethical obligations exist concurrently because of the social makeup of the classroom participants. The nature of the obligation to the other changes as the students and the educator change in the presence of each other (Martinez-Brawley, 2001; Miehls and Moffatt, 2000; Moffatt et al., 2005). The ethical approach is defined by multiple intersubjectivities that coexist in the classroom setting rather than one universal, all-encompassing ethical framework (Askins, 2016; Askins and Blazek, 2017; Miehls and Moffatt, 2000). Ethics in the face of diversity and the obligation to the other takes into consideration those students disadvantaged by the institutional structure of the university, those whose voices are lost, and those who are not present (Butler, 2006b, 2006c; Miehls and Moffatt, 2000; A. Smith, 1997). Thus ethics is not solely the practices related to the treatment of each other but rather part of an intersubjectivity in which the macro and micro influences are present.

In Miehls and Moffatt (2000), we argued that we become constituted as beings through the interaction with the other. I contend that that is still important to the construction of the self and the other. We also argued for an openness that constantly reflects on our engagement in the process of substitution (Miehls and Moffatt, 2000). Upon further reflection, I believe the concept of the reflexive self is useful since it avoids the dangers of thinking associated with stable categorical modes of thinking or a preoccupation with stability. However, the paradigm of the reflexive self may be limited, since it does not fully consider how to face the precariousness of both the student and the educator. It seems important to further challenge concepts of self as we take into consideration cognitive and affective responses to the other. Judith Butler offers a means to think through the reconstitution of the self.

JUDITH BUTLER AND THE DISPOSSESSED SELF

As I outlined earlier, the reflexive self can be imagined as social in a manner that is congruent with the social-constructionist approaches to social work discussed in chapter 3. The reflexive self offers the professor a way to imagine a reconstruction of the professor self through the experience of the other. Butler (2006a, 2006b, 2006c) elaborates on the social impacts on the self in a way that is congruent with the social self, outlined in chapter 4, and the reflexive self, defined earlier in this chapter, but she pushes the tentative nature of the self further. In this section, I rethink the reflexive self in order to outline how educators can be aware of their own dispossession and that of others. I explore the concept of the *dispossessed self* in this section by discussing dispossession of the self and *coming undone*.

The reflexive self promotes a relations view of the self over the autonomous view of the self (Miehls and Moffatt, 2000; Moffatt and Miehls, 1999). Social construction of the self and

160

reflexivity have helped us to live with and understand living with discomfort and anxiety (Moffatt and Miehls, 1999; Witkin, 2012a). With these concepts of social construction and reflexivity in mind, educators can also become aware of their dispossession arising from social relations. A risk of not reflecting on our own dispossession is that we might blame students or the other not only for creating anxiety but also for creating feelings of alienation. We create the other as the enemy, the dangerous, and the suspect for a variety of reasons, including avoiding our own sense of precariousness (Butler, 2006a).

The Dispossessed Self: Dispossession and Vulnerability

Social work theorists have discussed becoming disoriented through involvement in relationships with students, loved ones, or service users in a manner that invites deep questioning of the self to the point of feeling unhinged. The influence of the relationship can be so intense that the educator becomes uncertain of the proper nature of their pedagogical tasks and roles (Kumsa, 2006, 2007, 2012, 2016; Mandell and Hundert, 2015; Todd, 2012; Wehbi, 2015). According to Butler, an openness to the other invites a disruption to the autonomous self that is in control,

> the thrall in which our relations with others hold us, in ways in that we cannot always recount or explain, in ways that often interrupt the self-conscious account of ourselves we might try to provide, in ways that challenge the very notion of ourselves as autonomous and in control. I might try to tell a story here about what I am feeling, but it would have to be a story in which the very "I"

161

who seeks to tell the story is stopped in the midst of the telling; the very "I" is called into question by its relation to the "Other," a relation that does not precisely reduce me to speechlessness, but does nevertheless clutter my speech with the signs of its undoing. I tell a story about the relations I choose, only to expose somewhere along the way, the way I am gripped and undone by those very relations. My narrative falters, as it must. (2006b, 23)

Based on this openness to the other, Butler (2006a, 2006b) talks of *coming undone*. As a mode of relation, the self is a way of being for the other but is also about being dispossessed and made vulnerable by the other. To come undone is to begin from the starting point of dispossession and vulnerability to imagine the self. We become aware of not only how we are being socially constituted but also how we are becoming undone by social relationships (Butler, 2006a, 2006b). To enrich the concept of the reflexive social self, the educator might imagine a self that is aware of its own dispossession, as well as that of others (Butler, 2006a, 2006b).

We become undone by each other, and if we avoid reflecting on this process, we are missing an element of our own and others' subjectivities (Butler, 2006b). Furthermore, the concept of dispossession also allows us to be open to the marginality of the other. In this case, the ethics of engagement is informed by imagining that the self that is created in relationships is tied to those who are also dispossessed; the self becomes defined and reconstructed by marginality through race, class, gender, sexuality, and ability. When we are fully aware of this marginalization, we know that just relationships come not from treating each other in the same manner but rather from imagining relationships that have not yet come into existence. We avoid the mistaken beliefs that the other has a core quality that is the same as something within us and that people become present in the same manner if ascesis occurs within the universally defined concepts of justice (Butler, 2006b; Healy, 2005).

My social work classes are made up mostly of people who have been, and continue to be, vulnerable; thus, one can argue that the students are politically connected through their vulnerability. In particular, women, queer students, racialized students, Aboriginal students, and gender-diverse students are exposed to violence and assault inside and outside the classroom. We are attached to one another in the context of risk. Because of the possibility of social violence, our selves become a site of exposure while also involving articulation and assertiveness (Butler, 2006a). The self is not made present socially in a manner that is whole; rather, the social presence or ascesis of the self leads to exposure, risk, and pressures from social relationships.

I remember the genderqueer student who, when shown an image of the long line of refugees who were heading into Europe from Muslim countries, stated that his heart had been broken. He wished to go to Europe and be physically present with the refugee populations that were in flux and often turned away from the countries of the European Union. At the time, I thought his response was naïve, as it was not supported by sophisticated political and social interpretation. I now think that this was a clear expression of engagement through the politics of vulnerability and dispossession. This student was articulating a clear desire expressed through the awareness of dispossession and vulnerability when he was confronted with the dramatic image of the precariousness of the refugees in motion.

Instead of building an educational space of homeostasis focused on the intrapsychic self of the educator, or homeostasis

163

between community members, the classroom participants can openly build space and community based on the concepts of vulnerability (Mountz et al., 2015; Participatory Geographies Research Group, 2012) and loss (Butler, 2006b). Butler (2006b) argues that we should be open to coming undone rather than rushing to personal and interpersonal resolution that closes down discussion. In fact, she argues that significant political and social change can only occur through the disintegration of the self.

The Centrality of Loss and Mourning

According to Butler (2006a, 2006b), the experience of loss is central to being aware of disadvantage, social violence, and the vulnerability of others. In other words, with a heightened awareness of violence, we become aware of whom we have lost as educators and we become vulnerable to that loss. We also become aware of whom we do not hear from, as well as those people who are not present in the classroom. The educator, in this case, is concerned not so much with anxiety and homeostasis as with vulnerability and mourning, which leads the educator to come undone (Butler, 2006a, 2006b). I would add that this sense of loss is accentuated in the context of precarious existence discussed in chapter 1. Participants in my classroom have lost loved ones for reasons as wide ranging as AIDS, global conflict, police violence, addictions, and interpersonal abuse and violence.

In a classroom focused on social work and social justice, the participants experience a wide variety of types of loss that leads to mourning. We mourn the loss of hope brought about by the awareness of precariousness. We mourn the loss of our concrete sense of personal stability through the experience of social and economic fragility. We mourn our private, innocent, and well-meaning selves as they become sites of exposure. We also mourn the loss of freedom to express our desires in multiple possible ways, a constraint imposed by the dominant discourses. We mourn others who are close to us but remain outside the classroom as we discuss domestic violence, reactionary rage against immigrants, and religious intolerance. We mourn the deaths we experience in our marginalized communities, which are exposed to social, symbolic, and bodily violence. We mourn the absence of certain people in the classroom, whether their absence is the result of techniques of institutional exclusion, prejudicial relationships, or economic marginality.

I have argued in the past for a methodical working through with an attentiveness to change in direction (Moffatt, 1999b). This suggests that the focus of reflection is on my own temporary homeostasis. But to take Butler seriously, I might challenge myself to experience radical doubt in those moments when my self falls apart in the face of my students' precariousness and when I am mourning the absences in the classroom. Butler's attentiveness to the relationship to the other is similar to my attentiveness to the "in between" of relationships outlined in chapter 4, as well as the elusiveness of not knowing one's self or the other outlined earlier in this chapter and in chapter 1. The practice of reflection is challenged so that we can manage for a while, but we may find it difficult to continue as we become undone in the face of the other.

Each of us has also desired and loved (Butler, 2006b). From the point of view of the educator's reflexive social self, when I lose a person who is beloved, I also lose that part of the person that constitutes my self through its presence (Butler, 2006b;

Kumsa, 2006; Miehls and Moffatt, 2000). This type of loss is disruptive and destabilizing. When we allow ourselves to fully experience loss, we do not know what to do or who we are. Educators can become confused about who they are through the loss of the other and, therefore, can become inscrutable to themselves. Yet, according to Butler (2006b), when we fully experience loss, we engage in personal and social change. The desire for connection and sense of loss described earlier makes possible a community of meaning. This community of meaning, however, need not be summarized or described as a generalized whole (Butler, 2006b).

Social Engagement of the Dispossessed Self

In the past, I have been interested in a classroom process whereby I stay steady, stay the course, am methodical, and work through the process. Butler (2006a) challenges me instead to face the fact that it is possible to come totally undone as an educator. According to her, "When we are dispossessed from a community or a place, or when we lose people we are led to believe it is a temporary process of mourning we undergo. We assume order is to be restored" (2006b, 22). Butler (2006a) encourages educators to stick with the dissolution of the self in order to experience the delayed processes of mourning. In this manner, we face the fundamental dependency of human existence and our ethical responsibility that follows from it. Furthermore, Foucault (1972) challenges us to avoid privatizing grief or mourning because by personalizing and privatizing our emotions, we also participate in the act of depoliticizing social change.

A process based in loss can never be charted or planned, so it impossible to know in advance the result (Butler, 2006b). So too, the recognition of vulnerability based on an awareness of loss cannot be successfully resolved by replacing the other. For example, finding a new loved one does not resolve the mourning of a lost love. Replacement of others' bodies—for example, the replacement of the student by the professor's presence—is neither satisfying nor satisfactory (Butler, 2006b; Moffatt, 2001b; Moffatt et al., 2005). For those in marginal positions in the classroom, replacing their discourse and bodies with safer language only heightens the sense of loss (Moffatt, 2001b).

While imagining my self as completely open in cocreation with the other, I might also challenge myself to be fully attentive to the other's precariousness and suffering. Even as I feel my self as a site of exposure as the professor, I experience others' (the students') utter precariousness. This form of education cannot happen through a quick fix and an immediate answer. We do not want to jump to the type of quick conclusion found on the billboard outside Penn Station after the terrorist attack on the Twin Towers in New York, which proclaimed, "New York is stronger than ever."

Instead, we might think about loss as represented through the artist Felix Gonzalez-Torres's billboards in New York. An image of an empty, ruffled bed with two pillow imprints evokes the loss of his lover who died of AIDS. This image was mounted on twenty-four billboards across greater New York. There is no person in this artful image, which is meant to comment on loss and the erasure of life. Rather, the indent in the pillow on the empty bed suggests the loss of a person (Phillips, 2007). The symbol is constructed by an artist who experienced marginalization because of his HIV status, race, and sexuality. According to Phillips, with this image Gonzalez-Torres reminds us that "the physical manifestation of knowledge is a continuous process that rests in social relations rather than corporeal relations" (2007, 457). The image is free of commercial intent and open to process; it is open to suffering and affect and offers the possibility of multiple meanings. Suffering might lead to humility, unlike the other billboard mentioned earlier, that stating, "New York is stronger than ever," which is more likely to lead to angry retribution (Butler, 2006b).

While I need to be cautious of my claim that dissolution of the self provides a teachable moment, I do not share the same vulnerabilities as my students, and in many ways I do not have the same social risks. Encouraging dissolution of the self may simply be too much to bear for a student or colleague who is already experiencing precariousness. At the same time, as an educator, I feel that openness to the presence of the other, along with a refusal to be efficient in our responses, might lead to a productive emotional experience. Butler challenges us:

> Suffering can yield an experience of humility, of vulnerability, of impressionability and dependence and these become resources, if we do not resolve them too quickly; they can move us beyond and against the vocation of the paranoid victim who regenerates infinitely the justifications for war. It is as much a matter of wrestling ethically with one's own murderous impulses, impulses that seek to quell an overwhelming fear, as it is a matter of apprehending the suffering of others and taking stock of the suffering one has inflicted. (2006a, 149–150)

Butler's thought is in line with the social work literature based on the social nature of the self outlined in chapter 2, as it challenges us to consider a complete reconstitution of the self in the face of the other.

In an era of technological images, global awareness, provincial reactionary politics, and global violence, we can enrich the idea of ethical engagement as obligation to the other. The ethical task is to be attentive to the precariousness of the other and to the precariousness of life itself. In this case, ethical consideration begins with the questions, "Who counts as human? Whose lives count as lives? And finally, what makes for a grievable life?" (Butler, 2006b, 20). This does not involve simply reflecting on my own precariousness so that I can then understand another's precarious life. Rather, the precariousness of the other comes from the outside and disrupts the narcissistic circuit. We start our ethical task from a position of being undone (Butler, 2006a). According to Butler (2006b), that which is morally binding is not what comes from our own soul searching; it does not originate in my own autonomous reflexivity. In fact, moral obligation comes from elsewhere; it is unbidden and not planned. The moral obligation or the ethical imperative actually "ruins our plans" (Butler, 2006a, 131).

DISCUSSION

Some social workers continue to seek a foundational truth for social work, as well as a deliberate and universal plan. Yet no matter how well we organize the research of social work, and no matter how carefully we organize our interventions in a progressive, linear fashion, we can never fully plan for the exigencies of the loss of a sense of security. This is because personal identity and social precariousness are emotional in nature, so much so that a classroom can never fully be planned (Moffatt, 2001b). This inability of the educator to fully plan and control events in the classroom exists within the socioeconomic, political context of social precariousness. As Butler (2006b) says, to feel full emotional responses such as disillusionment or deep sorrow, we become foiled in our plans. Socioeconomic forces are larger than our choices, and they disrupt our deliberate projects. The abrupt and dangerous changes, the precariousness of social existence (Bauman, 2012), and our deep affective responses foil deliberate interventions and planning in our classrooms, as well as in social work practice, resulting in the necessity to engage in an ongoing form of reflexivity based on direct experience of the classroom.

The end of each term usually finds me feeling depressed and showing a lack of affect. It is as if I have flu-like symptoms, as I am weary both emotionally and physically. During this time, I separate from intense interpersonal relationships and interactions with my colleagues, as well as with the students in my classroom. I have in the past thought the source of depression was loneliness and isolation arising from a sudden loss of social stimulation. Now, I wonder whether this depression runs deeper and is a type of dissolution of the self. That self is tied to a wide range of affects, emotions, relationships, and components. The engaged social work professor who acknowledges intersubjectivity can no longer pretend to be neutral. The struggles of the students in our classrooms no longer can be viewed from a safe distance (Miehls and Moffatt, 2000).

Butler (1993, 1997) and Sedgwick (2003) have challenged my tendency to imagine myself in essentialist ways—that is, as a gay male from a working-class background. Gender, in particular, is not an essence embodied in our selves but rather is constructed socially. These female-identified authors have helped me to reflect on my faulty logic, which insists that as a man, I continue to be essentially the same after the term as I was during it. If I am always the same man at the end of term, then my loneliness is an affliction or a type of disease. If I am a man open to social relations and my masculinity is constituted socially, then my dispossession may involve a form of social engagement leading to change (Butler, 2006b; Laing, 2016). If I have been open to facing the many forms of both the personal and social precariousness of others, my end of term does not come to an affective resolution; rather, I have come undone because of my students' precariousness and suffering. I come undone because of the precariousness and suffering I witness on my way to work. I come undone because of the many forms of loss described earlier, including now the loss of my relationship with my students.

Butler (2006a) argues that we must also be open to that which comes unbidden and that which makes us feel as though we are falling apart through loss. A starting point for the constitution of the self is acute awareness of dispossession, social and physical violence, risk, and precariousness (Butler, 2006a, 2006b).

6

ARTS-BASED REFLECTION

I n this chapter, I argue that reflective practice includes affect and emotions, as well as cognition. Furthermore, I argue that we use an interdisciplinary arts-based approach to understand the importance of developing a social work literacy about images, as well as the artful presentation of the self. Emotions in this case become a resource rather than a complication in reflective practice. By using the concept of precariousness, I discuss how confusion, emotions, and indeterminacy are strengths of an arts-based approach to social work reflection.

ALLOWING SPACE FOR AFFECT AND EMOTIONS

I have argued in the past that the emotional reactions in the classroom are based not solely on the content of the course but also on the social dynamics of the classroom. At the same time, I have assumed that broader social interactions, social prejudice, and power strategies inform classroom dynamics (Miehls and

Moffatt, 2000; Moffatt and Miehls, 1999). At other times, emotional responses such as horror and disgust might be experienced by students as they become aware of how they are complicit in troubling social relations (Moffatt, 2004). In addition to this understanding of emotions, I now imagine a more direct relationship between the social context and emotions in that social relations directly construct emotional reactions. For example, in the past, I thought classroom content such as trauma and violence would create associations and memories for students that led to reactions to emotionally charged material (Moffatt, Carranza, Lee, McGrath, and George, 2012). I still believe this is true, but I also think that emotions including shame, anger, anxiety, and depression are created by social structures, institutional structures, and interpersonal relations (Deleuze and Guattari, 1983, 1987; Kristeva, 1982, 2002b; McGrath, Lee, Moffatt, Carranza, and Lagios, 2015; Moffatt et al., 2018). In fact, the social and economic structures that create the social conditions of individualism and precariousness cause emotional reactions such as depression, anger (Cvetovich, 2011), worry, and anxiety (Barnoff and Moffatt, 2007; Moffatt et al., 2018). Shame, too, is an emotional state that is tied to the many ways that gender, race, ability, and sexuality are expressed through social relations (Kristeva, 1982, 2002b; Moffatt, 2004; Munt, 2008).

Theorists have suggested developing an alternative political position by starting from the point of view of how we feel. Ahmed (2004a, 2004b) argues that we can draw attention to oppressive conditions by attending to, and reflecting on, our emotional responses. An affective or emotional starting point for politics stands in tension with those master narratives or dominant discursive frames that demand a nonemotional and neutral response about the economy, capitalism, and globalization (Ahmed, 2004b;

174

Askins, 2016; Thien, 2005). In fact, Butterwick and Dawson (2005) argue that treating affective and emotional responses as if they existed outside the range of institutional structures and discourses of knowledge is a powerful form of hegemonic control. Affective and emotional engagement can be a starting point for a reflective approach to considering the politics of social relations (Moffatt et al., 2018).

Affect

Affect has been defined as the unconscious sensation that is registered internally before the use of language or symbol (Thien, 2005). In other words, it is an intensity that lies beyond conscious cognition and drives people forward (Gregg and Seigworth, 2010; Thien, 2005). Rather than being intrinsic to human nature, affect is constructed through, and in reaction to, social relations (Deleuze and Guattari, 1987; Gregg and Seigworth, 2010; Massumi, 2002; Moffatt et al., 2018; Sedgwick and Frank, 1995). Affect has been characterized as a nonlinear process that involves "coming-to-emotions" (Askins, 2016; Askins and Blazek, 2017) and can be in play even when students and educators are not fully conscious of its influence (D. Gould, 2009).

I have argued in chapter 4 that the classroom is made up of a number of elements rather than existing as a unitary whole. Affect can be attached to any one of these elements, including ideas, ambitions, activities, institutional discourse, and sensations, as well as to other affects (Sedgwick, 2003). In this way, affect, such as worry or anxiety, has a broad sweep that can lead one to feel it is omnipresent or that it can be experienced in the moment (Moffatt et al., 2012; Moffatt et. al., 2018). For example, the accelerated speed of practice, which leads to demands of increased efficiencies, the reductive measurement of human worth, and the valuation of people based on measures of outcome, contributes to an affect constructed by neoliberal thought and practices (Ahmed, 2004a; Broger, 2016; Moffatt et al., 2018). This type of network or economy of affect can lead a person to drives that are problematic for that person's well-being (Broger, 2016; Mountz et al., 2015; Moffatt et al., 2018).

By reflecting on affect, we can focus on small-scale description and analysis rather than being preoccupied with the broad structures of control and influence that lie outside the classroom (Stern, 2012). The educator can critically interrogate how affect circulates in relationships and is experienced in the body (Askins and Blazek, 2017). At a time when neoliberalism is so pervasive and capital is so influential that we cannot discern their discrete influences on our lives (George, Moffatt, Alphonse, et al., 2009; Moffatt et al., 2018), reflecting on our affect can help us overcome immobilizing structural social forces and taken-for-granted values such as individualism and competition in order to reveal social realities that have been obscured (Ahmed, 2004a; Moffatt et al., 2018). So too, this approach helps us avoid a singular interpretation of life events.

Emotions: Bringing Affect to Consciousness

Emotions have been described as that stage of the affective process when one becomes conscious of one's feelings. Since emotions are tied to our reflective awareness in this manner, they underpin politics that can lead to action (Askins and Blazek,

2017) According to Askins and Blazek (2017), emotions are individual while existing in particular relational contexts across space. At the same time, they are contradictory since they can seem absent and obscure even while they are inscribed in our work and practices (Davidson, Bondi, and Smith, 2014). Davidson et al. argue that emotions are "intensively extensive, taking up all kinds of space and demanding *work*, concentrated collaborative efforts to be explored and understood" (2014, 1). The emotions of worry and anxiety, for example, become moments of self-conscious reflection about the forces shaping the university and the political nature of collegial and student-professor interpersonal relationships (Moffatt et al., 2018).

Reflective practice that focuses on emotions can pinpoint, describe, and create strategies to counter neoliberalism or other troubling dominant discursive frames. D. Gould (2009) has argued that the acknowledgment of emotions is a differing starting point for knowing from the rational point of view. If we start with emotional engagement, we avoid the "excesses of rationalist paradigms" in social sciences (Gould, 2009, 16). Reflective practices based on emotional responses work as a form of social justice practice in which we imagine how to change the context, as well as specific institutional and interpersonal politics (Askins, 2016; Barnoff and Moffatt, 2007; Fook and Napier, 2000; Moffatt, 2017). Thien states, "We are intimately subjected by emotion" (2005, 453). Since emotions reveal relationships, we address the everyday and specific life of emotion by understanding the intersubjective process (Moffatt et al., 2018; Thien, 2005). In this way, drawing on emotions can contribute to an analysis based on the history of the present, outlined in chapter 1. Reflection on emotional responses such as shame also can lead to the formation of communities of identity based on the constitution of emotions in the context of social relations (Moffatt, 2012d; Munt, 2008; Parada et al., 2010; Sedgwick, 2003).

Educators are aware of the multiscalar reality within which their emotional reactions exist. They understand that their emotions, practices, and roles are influenced, if not formed by, broader social and institutional relationships (Moffatt et al, 2018; Mountz et al., 2015; Participatory Geographies Research Group, 2012). Specifically, social work professors worry about restricted budgets, increasing efficiencies, and lost jobs that diminish the scholarly community. They also worry about an increasing culture of competition in which some succeed and others fail in the institutional context, where labor value is quantitatively measured through matrices of productivity (Moffatt et al., 2018). Furthermore, social work educators worry about surveillance and the centralization of power in higher levels of institutional governance, which leads to a decrease in autonomy (Moffatt et al., 2018).

Worry and anxiety are also emotional states that, if revealed, experienced together, and reflected on, might move us from paranoid victims to actors (Butler, 2006a) and help form practices that work against the effects of neoliberal restructuring (Moffatt et al., 2005; Moffatt et al., 2018). From this reflection on affect and emotion, it becomes possible to create spaces that foster a broader range of emotions and to open up a place for a passion for education and learning (Moffatt et al., 2018; Todd et al., 2015). Reflecting on emotions can lead to forms of resistance that include working collaboratively to create spaces free from worry and working together to avoid co-optation by broader discursive structures (McGrath et al., 2015; Moffatt et al., 2005; Moffatt et al., 2012; Moffatt et al., 2018). We can learn about social relationships by reflecting on the emotional effects engendered by oppressive circumstances and relationships (Ahmed, 2004b; Cvetkovich, 2011). In the last few weeks of each academic term, I feel quite anxious. Anxiety seems to be omnipresent in our classrooms as grades are given to the students, final assignments are due, and the end of term is imminent. This tension is tied to the competitive educational environment that is constructed based on meritocracy. It arises in response to the valuation and categorization of students through grades. Through this reductive measure, students get a sense of whether they are worthy enough of the university that they can proceed to further education. During this time, I remind myself that this palpable sense of anxiety is both personal and shared (McGrath et al., 2015; Moffatt et al., 2012). Because of my emotional response, the work of teaching seems overwhelming and the academic term feels too long. At times, my affective state and emotions make the work of being an educator seem unendurable (Moffatt, 2004; Moffatt et al., 2018). There is much to lose if an educator or student does not "make the grade." As discussed in chapter 1, we are anxious because each of us is "staving off the fall" (Bauman, 2012, 32). Our emotions are informed by the meritocracy tied to capitalism, which reminds us that some of us will be left behind while many of us are striving to overcome social precariousness (Moffatt, 2006).

An open cognitive approach tied to emotional engagement is a continuous reflexive process that is more akin to art than to science (Martinez-Brawley, 2001). Furthermore, an openness to endless reflexivity (Kristeva, 2002c; Kumsa, Chambon, Yan, and Maiter, 2015; Martinez-Brawley, 2002) creates an emotional dissonance in social work academia and a contradiction for students and educators (Kumsa et al., 2015). We engage students in this ongoing form of reflexivity, which is not easily resolved, yet limit the term to twelve weeks within which to express such reflection academically. The final grade the student receives at the end of term suggests a completion of learning and resolution of the self that is never possible since, as discussed in chapter 5, revealing the self is a task that is necessarily ongoing and incomplete. Yet it is possible to achieve the positive outcome of introducing emotional learning, since to start from the "irrational," or from our affect and emotions, might help us to evade the micromeasurements and precise disciplinary techniques of new managerial approaches to education (Martinez-Brawley and Zorita, 2007; Moffatt et al., 2018; Todd et al., 2015).

AN ARTS-BASED APPROACH
TO SOCIAL WORK

The psyche defined through attachment and symbol creation, discussed in chapter 5, and feelings-based engagement tied to affect and emotions, discussed earlier, invite an interdisciplinary arts-based approach to the field of social work. Coupled with the importance of reflecting on how affect and emotions are created socially is the need to reflect on those images discussed in chapter 3. An arts-based approach to reflective practice offers a wide enough scope to consider emotions, attachments, images, and symbols (Cramer, McLeod, Craft, and Agnelli, 2018; Phillips, 2007; Wehbi et al., 2018). In addition, emotional engagement that is not fully resolved invites an artistic expression of the self (Foucault, 1997a; Irving, 2014).

In the field of social work, there has been a long historical preoccupation with categorical approaches to social relations. For example, the field has had enduring categories of intervention referred to as the micro, mezzo, and macro levels of practice. Another differentiation in social work has been the parallel development of the community stream of practice and the interpersonal or therapeutic stream of practice. Finally, the policy level of practice has been defined as a type of expertise separate from and often elevated above direct intervention. These tidy characterizations of practice are the type of self-referential forms of thinking that are challenged by Michel Foucault as well as Gilles Deleuze and Félix Guattari.

Another thread of thinking within the social work profession values an open, interdisciplinary approach that allows for the creative imagining of social affairs (Cramer et al., 2018; Gray and Webb, 2008; Healy, 2005; Hyatt, 2014; Irving, 1994, 1999, 2014; Kim, 2017; Kumsa, 2016; Todd, 2005, 2012). There has also been an enduring historical discussion characterizing social work as an art rather than a science (Gray and Webb, 2008; Martinez-Brawley and Zorita, 2007; Moffatt, 2001a; Wehbi, Preston, et al., 2016). The artful exercise of teaching and practice works against a categorical or singular explanation of an event or a social work practice (Irving and Moffatt, 2002; Irving and Young, 2012; Todd, 2012; Trevelyan et al., 2012). Art, whether created within the classroom to fulfill a requirement for a course or introduced as material for study, can provide a catalyst for processes of critical reflection (Cole, 2017; Cramer et al., 2018; Kim, 2017; Moffatt, 2017; Wehbi, 2015; Wehbi, McCormick, et al., 2016; Wehbi, Preston, et al., 2016).

Social work is well suited to the concept of the multiscalar, with its focus on the importance of social context and social effects on microrelationships. As discussed in chapter 4, teaching and learning practices in the social work classroom, as well as social work practice in general, exist through components or traces of everything from the economy, politics, the state, and prejudicial relations defined by race, class, gender, sexuality, ability, and culture. Additional trace elements within practice include emotions, affect, personal and social history, identity, and the self. A certain combination of these traces or multiplicities becomes part of each of our practices and experiences. This multiplicity within the social work approach to practice defies the categorical approach to social work practice and instead invites an artful approach that is open to subjectivity, the poetic combination of elements, and unresolved experiences (Deleuze and Guattari, 1987; Irving, 1999, 2014; Irving and Moffatt, 2002; Kumsa, 2006; Moffatt, 2001a; Todd, 2012; Todd et al., 2015; Trevelyan et al., 2012).

The reflective arts-based approach to teaching social work allows for imagination that lies outside existing structures of language and normative discourses (Cole, 2017; Todd, 2012; Wehbi, 2015; Wojnarowicz, 2018). In other words, an arts-based approach allows for communication that is unbridled by taken-for-granted discursive frames and institutional restrictions. The meaning of dominant, enduring, and prevailing discourses can be unsettled, and new discourses might be co-constructed (Irving and Moffatt, 2002; Irving and Young, 2002; Moffatt, 2012b; Todd, 2012; Wehbi, 2015; Wojnarowicz, 2018). Furthermore, the co-creation and introduction of new discourses is open to the unexpected and ambivalent in a manner that runs counter to positivist and managerial approaches to knowing (Cole, 2017; Gray and Webb, 2008; Trevelyan et al., 2012; Wehbi, Preston, et al., 2016). Arts-informed teaching and social analysis can make the familiar seem unfamiliar, thus opening up space for knowledge construction, creative formation of the self, and reflective questioning (Irving, 1999, 2014).

As discussed in chapter 3, Foucault has argued that the care of the self, or ascesis, is a social practice rather than a solitary one. Ascesis is "the work that one performs on oneself in order to transform oneself or make one appear" (Foucault, 1997a, 137). Foucault documented the care of the self through archival research that found evidence of historical social practices that bring attention to bear on the individual (Halperin, 1995). Making one's self present can be a form of art (Irving, 1994; Irving and Moffatt, 2002; Irving and Young, 2002; Paton, 2015). Through this exercise, a postmodern politics of change becomes possible, a politics that includes the emotional, cognitive, and bodily reactions to making one's self present in a manner that is open to social relationships in the classroom (Irving and Moffatt, 2002; Irving and Young, 2002; Moffatt, 2012b; Todd, 2012). Through this artful approach to practice, students and educators can be creative in practice and become aware of how they construct each other and craft themselves through relationships to others in the classroom (Todd, 2012). By imagining an artful presentation of the self, we can discuss our own preferred relations with imagination and we can critically reflect on the expectations for others that we have put in place in the classroom (R. Jackson et al., 2015; Moffatt, 2001b, 2004; Moffatt and Miehls, 1999; Todd, 2012).

It is worthwhile to have a reflective discussion of the type of presence we as professors are encouraging and at times demanding in the classroom (Irving and Moffatt, 2002; Irving and Young, 2002; Miehls and Moffatt, 2000; Witkin, 2012a). By working through image and text in a thoughtful, reflective manner, we can interlink our smallest personal gesture with the broadest concerns of social justice (Moffatt, 2012b, 2012d; Wehbi, Preston, et al., 2016). Still, the way we make our selves present may not be definitive or easily understood if we need to imagine ourselves outside dominant discourses; art is a means to address the discourse of the self through an analysis of power, subjectivity, and knowledge creation (R. Jackson et al., 2015).

Arts-based inquiry opens up spaces for meaning making and interpretation that demand active creativity in terms of knowledge construction (Phillips, 2007; Trevelyan et al., 2012; Wehbi, 2015). The introduction of art in the classroom is one way that students can explore issues of knowledge creation, power relations, and subjectivity (Phillips, 2007; Sinding and Barnes, 2015; Trevelyan et al., 2012; Wehbi, 2015; Wehbi et al., 2018; Wehbi, Preston, et al., 2016). Furthermore, an arts-based approach to education invites an analysis and reconstitution of the interplay of knowledge, power, and subjectivity so that intrapsychic exploration is tied to the broader social context, thus enabling meaning making (Leonard, Hafford-Letchfield, and Couchman, 2018; Moffatt, 2016; Sinding and Barnes, 2015; Todd, 2005, 2012). Through art forms, we may also work through attachment and symbol creation in the development of the self and creating new meaning, as discussed in chapter 3. Art is a means to discuss the nature of truth and whether a truth claim is true or false. It can be a form of archival research that makes us question the meaning of evidence (Cole, 2017; Moffatt, 2017; Wehbi, Preston, et al., 2016).

The result of the foregoing analysis can be unsettling, since it engages students and educators in uncomfortable experiences and difficult emotions (Doyle, 2013; Trevelyan et al., 2012; Wehbi et al., 2018). The arts help us reflect on those difficult feelings and emotions (Doyle, 2013; Laing, 2016; Miehls and Moffatt, 2000; Todd, 2012; Trevelyan et al., 2012; Webbi et al., 2018). Trevelyan et al. argue that art can present "social work audiences with 'felt difficulty,'" which, in turn, is the "catalyst of all processes of reflexivity" (2014, 23). Todd (2012) notes that anxiety is tied to the discomfort of difficult learning. In fact, art, too often associated with or characterized as the "soft side" of practice, is part of the experience of artful social work practice that it is both "hard and soft" and involves struggle (Gray and Webb, 2008).

The arts can provide a voice for those who have been erased from the public realm, whether that realm is the interpersonal space of the classroom or the virtual space of media (Butler, 1993, 1997; Kristeva, 2006a; Wehbi, Preston, et al., 2016). When members of marginalized communities create their own images and cultures (Moffatt, 2012a, 2012b, 2012d), they become present and socially articulate their reality (Moffatt 2012a, 2012d; Sinding and Barnes, 2015; Wehbi, 2015). As Butler states, "Those who gain representation, especially self-representation, have a better chance of being humanized, and those who have no chance to represent themselves run a greater risk of being treated as less than human, regarded as less than human, or indeed, not regarded at all" (2006a, 141).

Butler (1997) imagines discourses taking on meanings when they circulate in contexts from which they have been barred or in which they have been unintelligible. Through the intervention of silenced or unintelligible discourses, a deconstructive politic intervenes to unsettle hegemonic meanings (Butler, 1997). While engaging in a performative politics, the students disrupt the hegemonic, they make utterable those who are not present, and in many cases, they see the possibilities of practices of their selves.

Ideally, arts practices in social work have a political purpose resulting in the transformation of social reality (Gray and Webb, 2008; Sinding and Barnes, 2015). In a time of precariousness, our education is enriched by exploring multiple disciplines to inform the many dimensions of human experience. Art, poetry, literature, drama, history, and philosophy provide modes of understanding that guide us through provisional reflection while we attempt to address sweeping concepts such as human suffering and human rights (Irving, 1994, 1999, 2014; Irving and Moffatt, 2002; Kumsa, 2016; Leonard et al., 2018). Art also allows one to address the limits of thinking, the liminal understanding of ever-changing social experiences, and secrets about difficult social relations, which leads to a new understanding of cultural space (Moffatt, 2012a). The hope is that through art we can evoke, imagine, and practice rehumanized social relations that lead to cultures open to justice and hope (Moffatt, 2012a, 2016; Sinding and Barnes, 2015).

Image Construction and Literacy: Navigating a Proliferation of Images

We are always faced with an excess of images and language (Derrida, 1997; Todd, 2007), yet the meanings available to us through these many images have been constricted (Kristeva, 2002c). A postmodern reflective social work approach questions the way in which such images act as normative schemes of that which is intelligible (Butler, 2006a; George, Moffatt, Barnoff, et. al., 2009; Irving, 1999, 2014; Lessa, 2006; Wehbi, 2015). At times, contemporary images are presented as if the humans were complete rather than contingent and unknowable (Kristeva,

1995). In this manner, these images act as norms of intelligibility and establish "what will and will not be human, what will be a livable life, what will be a grievable death" (Butler, 2006a, 146). The profusion of images we draw on on the internet cannot automatically be seen as a boundless resource for teaching and creativity. Rather, the profusion of images may be a box within which we have been trapped. Through reflection, we can intervene in the desensitizing "dream machine" that is the media (Apel, 2015; Butler, 2006a, 149). As educators, we can be alert to the two forms of normative power: one that produces the image of people as inhuman in order to foreclose understanding of the people and the groups they represent, and one that achieves the radical erasure or absence of people through a lack of images as if they never existed in the first place. In the second case, the public realm of appearance and images is constituted as the basis of exclusion. Since what can appear and who is heard are regulated, we need to reflect on the cry of emotions discussed earlier through this web of images and appearances (Butler, 2006a).

Normative schemes not only produce ideal images of what it is to be human but also produce images that illustrate people who are "less than human." Commercial imagery and media create the bounds of acceptable representation. Media have defined the representation of who is evil and who is the enemy. Images of the "enemy" represent a shifting target that is sometime female, sometimes Muslim, sometimes queer, sometimes disabled, and sometimes black. The image of the other is purposeful, since "we personify the evil or military triumph through a face that is supposed to be, to capture, to contain the very idea for which it stands. . . . The face here masks the sounds of human suffering and the proximity we might have to the precariousness of life itself" (Butler, 2006a, 145).

At other times, normative structures of commercial imagery do not provide an image at all, so that there has been no narrative of and no name for certain groups of people (Butler, 2006a). With a dearth of images with which marginalized people can identify, or through the absence of images that acknowledge their existence, marginalized people become invisible (Butler, 2006a). From a reflective approach to education, we can correct for the processes that lead to social violence and to invisibility, absence, and vulnerability.

As discussed in chapter 3, masculinist, gendered tendencies in image creation represent some humans, especially men, as pure, clean, and intact (Kristeva, 1982; Moffatt, 2004, 2012c; Butler, 2006a). With the demand for "true images," we must not simply change the image or make more images but instead challenge the presentation of reality. Media use has a propensity to close the meaning of the image (Kristeva, 2002c). Educators and students need to try to get outside these "closed" images to reflect on the incomplete image, the fractured thought, and the confusing social relationship. Media often represent a "perfect face" with which we cannot identify. At times, images seem to stop the flow of life. At other times, they whitewash the tensions associated with a sense of precariousness.

In order to represent people in a humane manner, the image must not only fail but also show how it is failing—that is, it must show how it has failed to fully capture the human. An image, therefore, should attempt to capture its referent (Butler, 2006a). Most importantly, we need to ask what grief and pain commercial imagery covers up or how those images help us to distance ourselves from the anxieties associated with neoliberal precariousness (Apel, 2015; Butler, 2006a).

With the exponential growth of social media and technological communication, we are self-conscious about how we present ourselves. It can be argued that through the use of social media platforms such as Facebook, Instagram, Twitter, and Snapchat, we curate a form of the self. This mediated expression of the self can be controlled and contrived. Depending on the social media platform, we think about the imagined audience and the message we wish to communicate. We pose ourselves in precise ways, we choose settings within which to be seen, and we choose whom we are shown with. In this manner, we voluntarily construct even the smallest of gestures for social consumption and construct meaning about our selves through these gestures. We are involved in these mediated expressions of the self through technology in the context of a broader sociocultural context of exposure and surveillance (Franklin, 1999).

DISCUSSION

We, as educators, need to be careful not to disrupt the difficult work of reflective practice we require of students, which involves working through affect or drive and emotions. We need time to reflect on how symbols affect us and the students emotionally, even while those emotions disrupt the pattern or grammar of the symbols. If professors are conscious of these needs, students may have the opportunity to encounter the uncomfortable and the unknown. These metamorphoses of the self in the classroom run counter to the commercial imagery of advertising that infiltrates public spaces and the media (Kristeva, 1995). For myself, the conditions that have allowed for the experience of psychic change

189

have mostly occurred outside the academic and commercial contexts. Such places include my father's car, a dance club, an artists' retreat, and a small, not-for-profit artists' gallery. It is possible, through reflective practice, for students to create symbols of subversion that disrupt or challenge the commercial symbols and open spaces of emotional attachment that are the beginning space for social politics. Reflective social work practice is an intuitive and creative process that embraces all aspects of the self, including the emotional and a multiplicity of truths (Fook and Napier, 2000; Gardiner, 2012; Napier and Fook, 2000).

7

REFLECTIVE POSTMODERN SOCIAL WORK IN THE CONTEXT OF PRECARIOUSNESS

I have argued that we live in a time of precariousness marked by uncertainty and change. Precariousness is created by a social and economic system built on principles of inequality, vulnerability, and exclusion. This book is a postmodern meditation on reflective social work practice and education. Postmodern social work also invites us to rethink the traditional social work categories, such as the clinical, community, and policy levels of practice (Witkin, 2014a). By giving up on categorical thinking, reflective practitioners are able to be open to many forms of truth, including knowledge creation through inductive approaches tied to direct experience (Fook and Gardner, 2007; Moffatt, 1999b; Napier and Fook, 2000). The postmodern approach also invites us to avoid a deductive approach to education (Napier and Fook, 2000) so that we can reflect on the elusive, nonreductive, and not easily measured components of social work practice, such as desire, affect, and attachment. Social relations from a postmodern perspective are constitutive of the self and interpersonal relations rather than being defined structures separate from practice (Irving, 2014; Witkin, 2014a). Furthermore, postmodern reflective practice includes direct experience, autoethnography, and narrative as important elements of social work. This approach to practice avoids technical approaches to knowledge that are separate from lived reality (Fook, 1999, 2002; Fook and Napier, 2000; Hyatt, 2014). In this manner, social work practice can be conceptualized so that rationalist, masculinist paradigms and technological interpretations of human affairs are open to reflective processes (Moffatt, 2012c).

POSTMODERN REFLECTION AND KNOWLEDGE CREATION

As discussed in chapter 1, we live in a world of continuous slippage where lived experience is no longer congruent with universal and controlled, categorical ways of thinking. In fact, arguments based on the assumption of stability and security too often are closed or self-referential metanarratives about the nature of social existence. These narratives, while attempting to reassure us that we live in a stable time, in fact obscure the precariousness of social life and the increasing tenuousness of the social safety nets that support public welfare.

From a postmodern point of view, knowledge and thought are socially constructed, with all the dangers and possibilities that accompany the social construction of knowledge. Through a reflective process, we move beyond dominant discursive structures in the social sphere in order to imagine new ways to think about and promote social change. Postmodern reflection is focused on all forms of knowledge construction, whether a completely formed ontology, a fully formed thought, or a fragment of thought that is not fully developed. This openness to a variety of forms of thought means we, as educators, are not always certain of our answer. Through reflection, educators can avoid becoming stuck in our truth claims. In fact, at times, we might publicly acknowledge that our thought has not been fully developed or has been incorrect.

The postmodern approach allows us to avoid misguided attempts to find a single, unitary, and foundational explanation in the social and economic context of capitalism and neoliberalism. The discursive frames tied to capitalism are contradictory, since they are presented as fully formed, separate ideologies outside the constraints of historical relationships yet are entrenched in networks of power and knowledge so that they saturate every relationship. At the same time, such economic structures are based on principles of insecurity and constant change. Since it is difficult to plan in the long term in the neoliberal environment, reflection allows us to continue to reflect on the critical analysis of social and economic systems as we move through them. We can think through and act on troubling social relations in order to imagine new social possibilities and different knowledge to promote social change that considers equality and equity.

The promulgation of a singular point of view with respect to social justice is a particular temptation in the context of so much uncertainty and the tentative nature of interpersonal and social relations. Furthermore, it is tempting for educators to search for a summary viewpoint when faced with increasingly large classes while being engaged in issues tied to teaching and practicing social change. The structure of the room, the use of technology, and the push for certain teaching outcomes all lead educators to focus outward with a desire to change the minds of their students. This book argues for the importance of using a reflective-practice stance to turn the gaze on our selves as educators and not slip into metanarrative or distancing techniques when engaged with students.

Throughout the book, I have argued that there is strength in social work when it draws on multiple forms of knowledge based on different social experiences. This awareness of multiple forms of knowing helps us become aware of the limits of knowledge. It also allows us to reflect on how knowledge may contribute to exclusion so that certain voices are not heard in the classroom. Furthermore, I have argued that a multiplicity of knowledge forms based on interdisciplinarity and arts-based approaches strengthens our ability to work through processes that imagine social justice. In order to be open to the ethical focus on precariousness, and the voice of the marginalized other, the reflective educator needs to focus on shifting meanings based on shared reflection rather than a singular point of view (Hyatt and Good, 2017; Mandell and Hundert, 2015; Napier and Fook, 2000).

USING REFLECTION TO TROUBLE DISCOURSE

I have argued that students learn about personal and social change in a context of pervasive global commercialism and social disparity (Kristeva, 1995). I argue that we need to reflect on authoritative, dominant discourses or metanarratives and how they are delivered. I have discussed a variety of discourses present in the classroom as wide ranging as the discourses of capital and commercial enterprise, the historical discourses of benevolence, and the discourse of gender.

Specifically, I have discussed the discursive structures of technology, neoliberalism, and new managerialism tied to capitalism. Postsecondary educational settings manifest these discourses through a variety of policies and practices, such as those that frame education as a form of job creation based on the value of students as entrepreneurs. These neoliberal discourses insist on the importance of unbridled commercial change guided by innovation and the disruption of traditional modes of learning, which, in turn, has the ironic effect of further enhancing a sense of precariousness for educators and students. How discourses combine in the classroom, however, can be eccentric and can change from class to class, which allows us to imagine alternative discourses and forms of resistance (Moffatt et al., 2016; Moffatt et al., 2018; Preston and Aslett, 2014; K. Smith, 2007).

Reflective teaching comes with great responsibility when we are educating students who have been, and continue to be, marginalized by race, class, gender, sexuality, and ability. As educators, we can support students to reflect on how they construct subjectivity and to think through and feel their presence in the classroom. At the same time, students and educators can reflect on the attendant emotional risks. Confusion, anxiety, and fear may be the result of students making themselves and their ideas intelligible in a social environment (the classroom) where their voices have not been heard before. In many cases, students speak from their own subjectivity to explore the possibilities of practices of their selves as they have experienced social relations influenced by race, sexuality, ability, and gender. The student may try to risk discourses that have been barred in the classroom and in the broader social context (Butler, 1997; Youdell and Armstrong, 2011).

The goal of the capitalist neoliberal project is to have individuals take responsibility for their own disadvantages, as well

195

as to reconstruct the student as a competitive self (Gray et al., 2015). These influences are so pervasive that the student dedicated to social justice may have to risk making an utterance that runs counter to dominant discourses. The discursive environment that has created exclusions through strategic power relationships makes it difficult for students who have been excluded on the basis of race, class, gender, sexuality, or ability to find a way to express their voices or engage in autoethnography in the classroom. While being present as a student in the classroom through discourse and the expression of self is difficult, it is central to the process of meaning making that leads to positive social change. Often, these practices and discussions are complicated since they disrupt the taken-for-granted discourses that exist in the university classroom. Yet this is a strength of social work education and social work student practice.

MAKING ONE'S SELF PRESENT: PRECARIOUS CHANGE

The type of social work imagined in this book focuses on ascesis, or making oneself present. This form of personal presence is tied to networks of language, symbols, and knowledge as they are related to strategies of power (Sirotich et al., 2012). Our selves and our presence in the classroom are intimately tied to how we think about and act in social relations. As a result, when we ask students to reconsider thought and their subjective engagement in social issues, we are also asking them to reflect on networks of power, knowledge, and the self. At the same time, the self reveals itself in the context of shifting relationships; in fact, the act of making the self present changes the social context that contributes to the formation of the self in the first place. The risk that attends this reflective analysis is that students may feel that their identities are in a precarious state on the verge of collapse. We are involved in teaching an emotional and cognitive dance that is more artful than scientific. The student is charged in social work courses to imagine professional engagement with the client. In this manner, we are asking them to be engaged in the exercise of symbol creation about the client while becoming a subject in process as a social worker. Furthermore, social work, when defined as a person-centered profession, too often leads the educator to demand that the social work student report an appropriate affect with respect to social relations in order to be engaged in responsible citizenry and to promote social betterment. Yet our students live in the same capitalist, symbolic culture that creates the anxieties outlined in chapter 6. A principal task of the reflective educator becomes imagining a space to teach outside omnipresent mechanisms of control, surveillance, discipline, reductive measurement, and examination. The task for educators is to be involved in a self-reflective process that does not become solely self-referential and avoids distancing techniques such as the teaching postures of enlightenment and certitude, which are based on binaries that define enlightenment and certitude as positive, while tentative knowledge and practice are considered to be negative. In fact, for students who reflect deeply, not knowing and tentativeness are important resources in meaning making (Irving, 1994; Fook, 2011; Todd, 2005, 2012).

Students who have experienced marginalization know about personal and social precariousness through direct experience. Social work students often represent the populations that are precarious as a whole and that are disadvantaged specifically by identity. Reflective practice in a contemporary context increases an awareness of social precariousness tied to social identities for students at the moment they are learning about such precariousness. So, as students become aware of the context of precariousness tied to broad socioeconomic forces, it may heighten their sense of insecurity arising from previous experiences of exclusion. In this case, awareness leading to reflective practice is not necessarily a quick route to an answer but may heighten a person's sense of confusion. Feelings of anxiousness and outright fear may be increased through the student's growing awareness of the pervasiveness of social insecurity and precariousness tied neoliberal approaches to well-being.

EFFECTING PSYCHIC CHANGE

When we are asking for reflection as educators, we are asking students to personally change in a profound manner. It seems that we are asking them to engage in a form of personal change that, although not necessarily bad, can be experienced as a form of precariousness. In order for students to seek personal transformation tied to social transformation, we are asking them to reevaluate deeply held beliefs and highly valued thought, to overturn bias, and to change their cognitive structures based on emotional reactions to social pressures from within and outside the classroom. Furthermore, reflective practice is demanding, since we ask students to consider the limits of their social understanding, the limits of their social experience, and the limits of their ontological presuppositions. As I argued in chapter 5, the experience of becoming undone can be considered an act of social justice. The type of profound change educators demand may be experienced as a form of personal collapse with the possibility of opening up a process that leads to a renewed social integration of the self.

The reinvigorated voice of the student brought about through the changed psyche, the transformed personal self, and the self made present in the classroom might all be imagined as key concepts in reflective learning. This personal and social reconstitution is meant to lead to the reconstruction of troubling social relationships. It is hoped that the socially reconstituted self might lead to a socially reconstituted classroom based on principles of social equity and justice. The process is unending, nonlinear, and open to disruption and change.

In the context of the social construction of the self and personal relationships, we can reimagine, through reflection, ways to think about private psychic space in the classroom. Such reflection involves risk, confusion, anxiety, and tension for both the educator and the student. Educators can reflect on the ways they facilitate meditative space that eventually allows for reintegration of the self and the psyche. It can be argued that along with risk and the sense of precariousness outlined earlier, the educator and the student need a space free from harm. In order to allow for this psychic space, educators need to be critically reflective about the manner in which we discipline, surveil, and examine students. In addition, we need to reflect on how our own processes of making our selves present as educators affect the subjective intrapsychic work of the student (Deleuze and Guattari, 1983, 1987; Trevelyan et al., 2012).

Rather than train students to take on an untroubled, permanent, professional identity, educators may help students imagine a sense of self that is always in doubt and tentative in nature. The professor might promote reflective practice in which

REFLECTIVE POSTMODERN SOCIAL WORK

constant questioning is welcome. As I argued earlier, the self is never complete and is always *becoming* (Kristeva, 2000). The student might engage in a process of psychic development and creation of the self that is akin to a tentative identity. Students' identities are provisional since they are subjects in process as they move through the dialectic of the semiotic and the symbolic. At the same time, a type of mourning takes place as the dream of a certain, coherent self no longer seems possible (Butler, 2006c; Kristeva, 2000; Kumsa, 2007; Mandell and Hundert, 2015).

Social work is a field that is marked by practitioners' skill in process. At the same time, the pedagogical demands on students in the helping professions are best met by an educator who is aware of, and attentive to, the coexistence of multiple subjective processes in the classroom. Educators need to be present and reveal their selves in order to create the climate for postmodern political process. Engaged students are endlessly in transition, since they learn by being open to others while being destabilized by the presence of the other. In the best case, several particular, creative singularities or subjectivities, including those of the educator, emerge at once because the students are fully engaged in meaning making. It is through this reflective engagement by the students as subjects in process that the possibility of a social and political project is possible for them.

* * *

The reflective practice discussed in this book includes reflection on the psyche, the self, and social relations all at once. None of these targets of reflection exists before the others. When reflective social workers seek to think outside the dominant symbolic order, narratives, and constraining discourses, they are engaged in a form of resistance. Reflection occurs in the context of constantly critiquing large political and social forces of control and engaging in constant examination of the changing self. There is no clear outcome or final resolution of such reflection (Irving, 1999; Kristeva, 2002c; Kumsa et al., 2015; Martinez-Brawley, 2001). The specific nature of reflection allows us to promote measures of social justice manifested through practice, by changing the elements present in the classroom, and by disrupting the taken-for-granted.

The process of meaning making for both students and educators is rife with mistakes, uncertainties, and conflicts. This type of work is all the more demanding in the context of commercial contemporary urban life and the omnipresence of symbols that are closed to meaning making, which are meant to be consumed by a passive consumer. The difficulty of this type of work is increased still further in the social context, where each presentation of the self and each utterance is expected to be polished and perfect. The role of the educator needs to be sophisticated in order to cocreate the type of classroom where students and the educator can make mistakes, question discourse, and risk speaking while all remaining engaged (Burstow, 2008). We might create communities of reflection based on a history of the present focused on experiencing, taking note of, and rethinking our daily practices, symbols, and emotions.

Our teaching response is a delicate dance that allows for attachment and symbol creation by the students while avoiding disciplinary actions performed by the educator. Reflective knowing in the context of assemblage cannot be too tidy; otherwise, we may not adequately consider the wide variety of components that make up an educational space. The possibility of capturing the moment of intervention to promote change and the possibility of adequately mapping the components of assemblage seem to be elusive. Furthermore, it is impossible to experience a sense of completion tied to an educational process that is associational rather than developmental and does not come to a logical end.

We, as educators, are involved in the exciting, creative process of helping students reflect on the self and the subject in process that is attuned to the semiotic or affective sphere while becoming conscious of and adept at symbol creation. The participants in learning, including the educator and student, continue to risk reflecting on psychic change that is so disconcerting it may lead them to feel a personal sense of precariousness. This form of reflection is especially important for educators in postsecondary educational institutions, who are in strategic power relationships that promote dominant discourses that create social exclusion. Reflection that lies at the edge of self-expression and outside cognitive certainty is the way to find a process of resistance that can lead to reflective social change and supple expressions of social justice.

WORKS CITED

Abrams, L. S., & Moio, J. A. (2009). Critical race theory and the cultural competence dilemma in social work education. *Journal of Social Work Education 45*(2), 245–261.

Ahmed, S. (2004a). Affective economies. *Social Text, 22*(2), 117–139.

Ahmed, S. (2004b). *The cultural politics of emotions.* New York: Routledge.

Anderson, G. (2006). Carving out time and space in the managerial university. *Journal of Organizational Change Management, 19*(5), 578–592.

Apel, D. (2015). *Beautiful terrible ruins: Detroit and the anxiety of decline.* New Brunswick, N.J.: Rutgers University Press.

Argyris, C., & Schön, D. (1992). *Theory in practice: Increasing professional effectiveness.* San Francisco: Jossey-Bass. (Original work published 1974)

Aronson, J., & Sammon, S. (2000). Practice and social service cuts and restructuring: Working with the contradiction of small victories. *Canadian Social Work Review, 17*(2), 167–187.

Askeland, G., & Fook, J. (2009). Critical reflection in social work. *European Journal of Social Work, 12*(3), 287–292.

Askins, K. (2016). Emotional citizenry: Everyday geographies of befriending, belonging and intercultural encounter. *Transactions of the Institute of British Geographers, 41*, 515–527.

Askins, K., & Blazek, M. (2017). Feeling our way: Academia, emotions and a politics of care. *Social and Cultural Geography, 18*(8), 1086–1105.

Baileyegu, W., Martin, S., Moffatt, K., Savaranamuttu, R., Ruhinda, S., . . . Vaz, J. (2000). *Reflecting on masculinity in a multicultural classroom*. Paper presented at the Joint Conference of International Federation of Social Workers and International Schools of Social Work, Montreal.

Baldwin, M. (2004). Conclusions: Optimism and the art of the possible. In N. Gould & M. Baldwin (Eds.), *Social work, critical reflection and the learning organization* (pp. 161–176). Aldershot, UK: Ashgate.

Ball, S. (2012). Performativity, commodification and commitment: An I-spy guide to the neoliberal university. *British Journal of Educational Studies, 60*(1), 17–28.

Ball, S., & Olmedo, A. (2013). Care of the self, resistance and subjectivity under neoliberal governmentalities. *Critical Studies in Education, 54*(1), 85–96.

Barnes, H. (2015). Performing understanding: Investigating and expressing difference and trauma. In C. Sinding & H. Barnes (Eds.), *Social work artfully: Beyond borders and boundaries* (pp. 115–133). Waterloo, Ontario: Wilfred Laurier Press.

Barnoff, L., & Moffatt, K. (2007). Contradictory tensions in anti-oppression practice in feminist social services. *Affilia: Journal of Women and Social Work, 22*(1), 56–70.

Bauman, Z. (2005). Education in liquid modernity. *Review of Education, Pedagogy, and Cultural Studies, 27*, 303–317.

Bauman, Z. (2011). *Collateral damage: Social inequalities in a global age.* Cambridge, UK: Polity Press.

Bauman, Z. (2012). *Liquid modernity.* Cambridge, UK: Polity Press.

Béres, L. (2012). Celtic spirituality and postmodern geography: Narratives of engagement with place. *Journal for the Study of Spirituality, 2*(2), 170–185.

Béres, L. (2014). *The narrative practitioner: Practice theory in context.* New York: Palgrave Macmillan.

Béres, L., Bowles, K., & Fook, J. (2011). Narrative therapy and critical reflection on practice: A conversation with Jan Fook. *Journal of Systemic Therapies, 30*(2), 81–97.

Bleakley, A. (1999). From reflective practice to holistic reflexivity. *Studies in Higher Education, 24*(3), 315–330.

Brandt, J. (2001). Revolt or consensus? Julia Kristeva in the 1990s. *L'Esprit Createur, 41*(1), 85–96.

Brehony, K., & Deem, R. (2005). Challenging the post-Fordist/flexible organisation thesis: The case of reformed educational organisations. *British Journal of Sociology of Education, 26*(3), 395–414.

Broger, K. (2016). The rule of mimetic desire in higher education: Governing through naming, shaming and framing. *British Journal of Sociology of Education, 37*(1), 72–91.

Bruneau, W., & Savage, D. (Eds.). (2002). *Counting out the scholars: The case against performance indicators in higher education.* Toronto: James Lorimer.

Bullen, E., Fahey, J., & Kenway, J. (2006). The knowledge economy and innovation: Certain uncertainty and the risk economy. *Discourse: Studies in the cultural politics of education, 27*(1), 53–68.

Burstow, B. (1991). Freirian codifications and social work education. *Journal of Social Work Education, 27*(2), 196–207.

Burstow. B. (2008). Invisible theatre, ethics, and the adult educator. *International Journal of Lifelong Learning, 27*(3), 273–288.

Butler, J. (1990). *Gender trouble: Feminism and the subversion of identity.* New York: Routledge.

Butler, J. (1993). *Bodies that matter: On the discursive limits of "sex."* New York: Routledge.

Butler, J. (1997). Critically queer. In S. Phelan (Ed.), *Playing with fire: Queer politics, queer theories* (pp. 11–29). New York: Routledge.

Butler, J. (2006a). Precarious life. In *Precarious life: The powers of mourning and violence* (pp. 128–151). New York: Verso.

Butler, J. (2006b). Violence, mourning, politics. In *Precarious life: The powers of mourning and violence* (pp. 19–49). New York: Verso.

Butterwick, S., & Dawson, J. (2005). Undone business: Examining the production of academic labour. *Women's Studies International Forum, 28*, 51–65.

Chambon, A. (1994). Postmodernity and social work discourse(s). In A. Chambon and A. Irving (Eds.), *Essays on postmodernism and social work* (pp. 63–72). Toronto: Canadian Scholars' Press.

Chambon, A. (1999). Foucault's approach: Making the familiar visible. In A. Chambon, A. Irving, and L. Epstein (Eds.), *Reading Foucault for social work* (pp. 51–82). New York: Columbia University Press.

Chambon, A., & Irving, A. (2003). "They give reason a responsibility which it simply can't bear": Ethics, care of the self, and caring knowledge. *Journal of Medical Humanities, 24*(3–4), 265–278.

Chambon, A., Irving, A., & Epstein, L. (Eds.). (1999). *Reading Foucault for social work.* New York: Columbia University Press.

Clarke, J. (2010). After neo-liberalism? Markets, states and the reinvention of public welfare. *Cultural Studies, 24*(3), 375–394.

Cleary, M., Horsfall, J., Happell, B., & Hunt, G. E. (2013). Reflective components in undergraduate mental health nursing curricula: Some issues for consideration. *Issues in Mental Health Nursing, 34*(2), 69–74.

Cole, K. (2017). Route of heroes. In S. Chambers, J. Farrow, M. FitzGerald, E. Jackson, J. Lorinc, T. McCaskell, . . . R. Thawer (Eds.), *Any other way: How Toronto got queer* (pp. 276–278). Toronto: Coach House Press.

Cramer, E., McLeod, D., Craft, M., & Agnelli, K. (2018). Using arts-based materials to explore the complexities of clinical decision-making in a social work methods class. *Social Work Education, 37*(3), 342–360.

Cvetkovich, A. (2011). *Depression: A public feeling,* Durham, N.C.: Duke University Press.

Davidson, J., Bondi, L., & Smith, M. (2014). An emotional contradiction. *Emotions, Space, Society 10*, 1–3.

Davies, B. (2005). The (im)possibility of intellectual work in neoliberal regimes. *Discourse: Studies in the Cultural Politics of Education, 26*(1), 1–14.

Deem, R. (2008). Unravelling the fabric of academe: The managerialist university and its implications for the integrity of academic work. In J. Turk (Ed.), *Universities at risk: How politics, special interests and corporatization threaten academic integrity* (pp. 256–281). Toronto: Lorimer.

Deem, R., Hillyard, S., & Reed, M. (2007). *Knowledge, higher education, and the new managerialism: The changing management of UK universities.* Oxford: Oxford University Press.

Dei, G. (2008). *Racists beware: Uncovering racial politics in contemporary society.* New York: Sense.

Deleuze, G. (1990). *Negotiations* (M. Joughlin, Trans.). New York: Columbia University Press.

Deleuze, G., & Guatarri, F. (1983). *Anti-Oedipus, capitalism and schizophrenia* (R. Hurly, M. See, & H. R. Lane, Trans.). Minneapolis: University of Minnesota Press.

Deleuze, G., & Guatarri, F. (1987). *A thousand plateaus: Capitalism and schizophrenia* (B. Massumi, Trans.). Minneapolis: University of Minnesota Press.

Derrida, J. (1997). *Politics of friendship* (G. Collins, Trans.). New York: Verso.

Dohn, N. B. (2011). On the epistemological presuppositions of reflective activities. *Educational Theory, 61*(6), 671–708.

Donovan, J., Rose, D., & Connolly, M. (2017). A crisis of identity: Social work theorising in a time of change. *British Journal of Social Work, 47*(8), 2291–2307.

Dosse, F. (2010). *Gilles Deleuze and Felix Guattari: Intersecting lives* (D. Glassman, Trans.). New York: Columbia University Press.

Doyle, J. (2013). *Hold it against me: Difficulty and emotion in contemporary art.* Durham, N.C.: Duke University Press.

Duval, J., & Béres, L. (2011). *Innovations in narrative therapy: Connecting practice, training, and research.* New York: Norton.

Eribon, D. (1991). *Michel Foucault* (B. Wing, Trans.). Cambridge, Mass.: Harvard University Press.

Fanghanel, J., & Trowler, P. (2008). Exploring academic identities and practices in a competitive enhancement context: A UK-based study. *European Journal of Education, 43*(3), 301–313.

Farrell, C., & Morris, J. (2003). The neo-bureaucratic state: Professionals, managers and professional managers in schools, general practices and social work. *Organizations, 10*, 129–156.

Fook, J. (1999). Critical reflectivity in education and practice. In B. Pease & J. Fook (Eds.), *Transforming social work practice: Postmodern critical perspectives* (pp. 195–210). New York: Routledge.

Fook, J. (2002). *Social work: Critical theory and practice.* Thousand Oaks, Calif.: Sage.

Fook, J. (2011). Uncertainty: The defining characteristic of social work? In V. E. Cree (Ed.), *Social work: A reader* (pp. 29–34). New York: Routledge.

Fook, J. (2012). The challenges of creating critically reflective groups. *Social Work with Groups, 35*(3), 218–234.

Fook, J. (2014). Learning from and researching (my own) experience: A critical reflection on the experience of social difference. In S. Witkin (Ed.), *Narrating social work through autoethnography* (pp. 120–140). New York: Columbia University Press.

Fook, J. (2016). *Social work: A critical approach to practice* (3rd ed.). London: SAGE.

Fook, J., & Askeland, G. (2007). Challenges of critical reflection: "Nothing ventured, nothing gained." *Social Work Education, 26*(5), 520–533.

Fook, J., & Gardner, F. (2007). *Practising critical reflection: A resource handbook.* New York: Open University Press.

Fook, J., & Kellehear, A. (2010). Using critical reflection to support health promotion goals in palliative care. *Journal of Palliative Care, 26*(4), 295–302.

Fook, J., & Napier, L. (2000). From dilemma to breakthrough: Retheorising social work. In L. Napier & J. Fook (Eds.), *Breakthroughs in practice: Theorising critical moments in social work* (pp. 212–227). London: Whiting and Birch.

Foucault, M. (1972). *The archaeology of knowledge and the discourse on language* (A. M. Sheridan Smith, Trans.). New York: Pantheon Books.

Foucault, M. (1973). *The order of things: An archeology of human science.* New York: Vintage.

Foucault, M. (1979). *Discipline and punish: The birth of the prison* (A. Sheridan, Trans.). New York: Vintage Books.

Foucault, M. (1980a). Body/power. In C. Gordon (Ed.), *Power/knowledge: Selected interviews and other writings, 1972–1977* (C. Gordon, L. Marshall, J. Mepham, & K. Soper, Trans.) (pp. 55–62). New York: Pantheon Books.

Foucault, M. (1980b). Power and strategies. In C. Gordon (Ed.), *Power/knowledge: Selected interviews and other writings, 1972–1977* (C. Gordon, L. Marshall, J. Mepham, & K. Soper, Trans.) (pp. 134–145). New York: Pantheon Books.

Foucault, M. (1980c). Prison talk. In C. Gordon (Ed.), *Power/knowledge: Selected interviews and other writings, 1972–1977* (C. Gordon, L. Marshall,

J. Mepham, & K. Soper, Trans.) (pp. 37–54). New York: Pantheon Books.

Foucault, M. (1980d). Truth and power. In C. Gordon (Ed.), *Power/knowledge: Selected interviews and other writings, 1972–1977* (C. Gordon, L. Marshall, J. Mepham, & K. Soper, Trans.) (pp. 109–133). New York: Pantheon Books.

Foucault, M. (1988a). *The history of sexuality: Vol. 3. The care of self* (R. Hurly, Trans.). New York: Random House.

Foucault, M. (1988b). On power. In L. D. Kritzman (Ed.), *Politics, philosophy, culture: Interviews and other writings, 1977–1984* (pp. 96–109). New York: Routledge.

Foucault, M. (1997a). Friendship as a way of life. In P. Rabinow (Ed.), *The essential works of Foucault, 1954–1984: Vol. 1. Ethics: Subjectivity and truth* (R. Hurly, Trans.) (pp. 135–140). New York: New Press.

Foucault, M. (1997b). Technologies of the self. In P. Rabinow (Ed.), *The essential works of Foucault, 1954–1984: Vol. 1. Ethics: Subjectivity and truth* (R. Hurly, Trans.) (pp. 223–251). New York: New Press.

Franklin, U. (1999). *The real world of technology*. Toronto: Anansi Press.

Freire, P. (1970a). *Cultural action for freedom*. London: Penguin Books.

Freire, P. (1970b). *The pedagogy of the oppressed* (M. B. Ramos, Trans.). New York: Continuum.

Gardner, F. (2012). The car, the rain, and meaningful conversation: Reflexivity and practice. In S. Witkin (Ed.), *Social construction and social work practice: Interpretations and innovations* (pp. 103–126). New York: Columbia University Press.

George, P., Moffatt, K., Alphonse, M., Kanitkar, A., Anand, V., & Chamberlain, J. (2009). Strategies of resistance in the context of marginalization and globalization in India. *Social Development Issues, 31*(3), 1–14.

George, P., Moffatt, K., Barnoff, L., Coleman, B., & Paton, C. (2009). Image construction as a strategy of resistance by progressive community organizations. *Revue Novelles Practiques Sociales, 22*(1), 92–110.

Gibson, M. F. (2015). Intersecting deviance: Social work, difference and the legacy of eugenics. *British Journal of Social Work, 45*(1), 313–330.

Ginsberg, B. (2011). *The fall of the faculty: The rise of the all-administrative university and why it matters*. Oxford: Oxford University Press.

Giroux, H. A. (1992). Paulo Freire and the politics of postcolonialism. *Journal of Advanced Composition, 12*(1), 15–26.

Gordon, C. (1980). Afterword. In C. Gordon (Ed.). *Power/knowledge: Selected interviews and other writings, 1972–1977* (C. Gordon, L. Marshall, J. Mepham, & K. Soper, Trans.) (pp. 229–260). New York: Pantheon Books.

Gosine, K., & Pon, G. (2011). On the front lines: The voices and experiences of racialized child welfare workers in Toronto, Canada. *Journal of Progressive Human Services 22*, 135–159.

Gould, D. (2009). *Moving politics: Emotion and ACT UP's fight against AIDS.* Chicago: University of Chicago Press.

Gould, N. (2004). Introduction: The learning organization and reflective practice—the emergence of a concept. In N. Gould & M. Baldwin (Eds.), *Social work, critical reflection and the learning organization* (pp. 1–10). Aldershot, UK: Ashgate.

Gould, N., & Baldwin, N. (Eds.). (2004). *Social work, critical reflection and the learning organization.* Aldershot, UK: Ashgate.

Gould, N., & Taylor, I. (Eds.). (1999). *Reflective learning for social work: Research, theory and practice.* Aldershot, UK: Ashgate.

Graham, M. J. (2017). *Reflective thinking in social work: Learning from student narratives.* New York: Routledge.

Granfield, D., & Moffatt, K. (2009). *Working with Wikipedia: A librarian/faculty collaboration.* Paper presented at the Ontario Library Association Super Conference, Toronto.

Grant, G. P. (1959). *Philosophy in the mass age.* Toronto: Copp Clark.

Gray, M., Dean, M., Agilias, K., Howard, A., & Schubert, L. (2015). Perspectives on neoliberalism for human service professionals. *Social Service Review, 89*(2), 368–392.

Gray, M., & Webb, S. (2008). Social work as art revisited. *International Journal of Social Welfare, 17*(2), 182–193.

Gregg, M., & Seigworth, G. (2010). *The affect theory reader.* Durham, N.C.: Duke University Press.

Halperin, D. (1995). *Saint Foucault: Towards a gay hagiography.* New York: Oxford University Press.

Hansen, T. B. (1997). Inside the romanticist episteme. *Thesis Eleven, 48*, 21–41.

Hare, I. (2004). Defining social work for the 21st century: The International Federation of Social Workers' revised definition of social work. *International Social Work, 47*(3), 407–424.

Hargreaves, J. (2010). Voices from the past. In H. Bradbury, N. Frost, S. Kilminster, and M. Zukus (Eds.), *Beyond reflective practice: New approaches to professional lifelong learning* (pp. 83–95). Abingdon, UK: Routledge.

Harms Smith, L., & Nathane-Taulela, M. (2015). Art towards critical conscientization and social change during social work and human rights education, in the South African post apartheid and post colonial context. In C. Sinding & H. Barnes (Eds.), *Social work artfully: Beyond borders and boundaries* (pp. 63–78). Waterloo, Ontario: Wilfred Laurier Press.

Hay, S., & Kapitzke, C. (2009). "Smart state" for a knowledge economy: Reconstituting creativity through student subjectivity. *British Journal of Sociology of Education, 30*(2), 151–164.

Healy, K. (2000). *Social work practices: Contemporary practices on change.* London: SAGE.

Healy, K. (2005). *Social work theories in context: Creating frameworks for practice.* New York: Palgrave Macmillan.

Healy, K., & Leonard, P. (2000). Responding to uncertainty: Critical social work in the postmodern habitat. *Journal of Progressive Human Services, 11*(1), 23–48.

Heron, B. (2005). Self-reflection in critical social work practice: Subjectivity and the possibilities of resistance. *Reflective Practice, 6*(3), 341–351.

Hickson, H. (2016). Becoming a critical narrativist: Using critical reflection and narrative inquiry as a research methodology. *Qualitative Social Work, 15*(3), 380–391.

Hyatt, E. D. G. (2014). From healer to transformed healer: Relearning lessons in grief. *Reflections: Narratives of Professional Helping, 20*(2), 32–41.

Hyatt, E. D. G., & Good, B. D. (2017). Supervisor and intern reflections on a year of research: Why it worked. *Reflections: Narratives of Professional Helping, 23*(1), 66–75.

Irving, A. (1994). From image to simulacra: The modern/postmodern divide and social work. In A. Chambon and A. Irving (Eds.), *Essays on postmodernism and social work* (pp. 21–34). Toronto: Canadian Scholars' Press.

Irving, A. (1999). Waiting for Foucault: Social work and the multitudinous truths of life. In A. Chambon, A. Irving, and L. Epstein (Eds.), *Reading Foucault for social work* (pp. 27–51). New York: Columbia University Press.

Irving, A. (2014). The pretty girl in the mirror: A gender transient's tale. In S. Witkin (Ed.), *Narrating social work through autoethnography* (pp. 260–283). New York: Columbia University Press.

Irving, A., & Moffatt, K. (2002). Intoxicated midnight and carnival classrooms: The professor as poet. *Radical Pedagogy, 4*(1). Retrieved from http:// radicalpedagogy.icaap.org/content/issue4_1/05_irving-moffatt.html

Irving, A., & Young, T. (2002). Paradigm for pluralism: Mikhail Bakhtin and social work practice. *Social Work, 47*(1), 19–29.

Jackson, R., Debassige, C., Masching, R., & Whitebread, W. (2015). Towards an Indigenous narrative inquiry: The importance of composite narrative representations. In C. Sinding & H. Barnes (Eds.), *Social work artfully: Beyond borders and boundaries* (pp. 135–158). Waterloo, Ontario: Wilfred Laurier Press.

Jackson, S. (2007). Freire re-viewed. *Educational Theory, 57*(2), 199–213.

Jorgensen, E. R., & Yob, I. R. (2013). Deconstructing Deleuze and Guattari's *A Thousand Plateaus* for music education. *Journal of Aesthetic Education, 47*(3), 36–55.

Julia Kristeva: Texts in English. (n.d.). Retrieved from http://www.kristeva .fr/english.html

Keenan, E., Miehls, D., Moffatt, K., Orwat, J., & White, J. (2004). Cacophony, polyphony or fugue: Exploring sociocultural concepts with social work students. *Smith College Studies in Social Work, 74*(2), 427–448.

Keenan, M. (2012). Opening a space for hope in a landscape of despair: Trauma and violence work with men who have sexually abused minors. In S. Witkin (Ed.), *Social construction and social work practice: Interpretations and innovations* (pp. 240–277). New York: Columbia University Press.

Kim, H. C. (2017). A challenge to the social work profession? The rise of socially engaged art and a call to radical social work. *Social Work, 62*(4), 305–311.

King, R. (2010). Policy internationalization, national variety and governance: Global markets and network power in higher education states. *Higher Education, 60*(6), 583–594.

Kinsella, E. A. (2007). Technical rationality in Schön's reflective practice: Dichotomous or non-dualistic epistemological positions. *Nursing Philosophy, 8*(2), 102–113.

Kinsella, E. A. (2010). Professional knowledge and the epistemology of reflective practice. *Nursing Philosophy, 11*(1), 3–14.

Koenig, T., Spano, R., Kaufman, D., Leiste, M., Tynyshbayeva, A., Mady-arbekov, G., & Karataevna-Makhadiyeva, A. (2017). A Freirean analysis of Kazakhstani social work education. *International Social Work, 60*(1), 156–169.

Kristeva, J. (1982). *Powers of horror: An essay on abjection* (L. S. Roudiez, Trans.). New York: Columbia University Press.

Kristeva, J. (1995). *New maladies of the soul* (R. Guberman, Trans.). New York: Columbia University Press.

Kristeva, J. (2000). *The sense and non-sense of revolt: The powers and limits of psychoanalysis* (J. Herman, Trans.). New York: Columbia University Press.

Kristeva, J. (2002a). *Intimate revolt: The powers and limits of psychoanalysis* (Vol. 2) (J. Herman, Trans.). New York: Columbia University Press.

Kristeva, J. (2002b). Julia Kristeva in conversation with Rosalind Coward (1984). In K. Oliver (Ed.), *The portable Kristeva* (pp. 333–350). New York: Columbia University Press.

Kristeva, J. (2002c). *Revolt, she said: An interview by Philippe Petit* (S. Lotringer, Ed.; B. O'Keeffe, Trans.). New York: Semiotext(e) Foreign Agents Series.

Kristeva, J., & Spire, A. (2003). The future of a defeat. *Parallax, 9*(2), 21–26.

Kritzman, L. (1988). Introduction: Foucault and the politics of experience. In L. Kritzman (Ed.), *Politics, philosophy, culture: Interviews and other writings, 1977–1984* (pp. ix–xxv). New York: Routledge.

Kumsa, M. K. (2006). "No! I am not a refugee": The poetics of be-longing among young Oromos in Toronto. *Journal of Refugee Studies, 19*(2), 231–255.

Kumsa, M. K. (2007). A resettlement story of unsettlement: Transformative practices of taking it personally. In D. Baines (Ed.), *Doing anti-oppressive practice: Building transformative politicized social work* (pp. 111–127). Halifax, Nova Scotia: Fernwood.

Kumsa, M. K. (2012). When woman at risk meets youth at risk: Engaging the discursive practices of the nation state. In S. Witkin (Ed.), *Social construction and social work practice: Interpretations and innovations* (pp. 308–334). New York: Columbia University Press

Kumsa, M. K. (2016). Thinking about research. *Qualitative Social Work, 15*(5–6), 602–609.

Kumsa, M. K., Chambon, A., Yan, M., & Maiter, S. (2015). Catching the shimmers of the social: From the limits of reflexivity to methodological creativity. *Qualitative Research, 15*(4), 419–436.

Laing, O. (2016). *The lonely city: Adventures in the art of being alone.* New York: Picador.

LaSala, M. (2013). Out of the darkness: Three waves of family research and the emergence of family therapy for lesbian and gay people. *Clinical Social Work Journal, 41*, 267–276.

Lee, B. (1999). *Pragmatics of community organization* (3rd ed.). Mississauga, Ontario: CommonAct Press.

Lee, B., McGrath, S., Moffatt, K., & George, U. (2002). Exploring the insider role in community practice within diverse communities. *Critical Social Work, 2*(2), 69–87.

Leonard, K., Hafford-Letchfield, T., & Couchman, W. (2018). The impact of the arts in social work education: A systematic review. *Qualitative Social Work, 17*(2), 286–304.

Lessa, I. (2006). Discursive struggles within social welfare: Restaging teen motherhood. *British Journal of Social Work, 36*(2), 283–298.

Macias, T. (2015). "Between a rock and a hard place": Negotiating the neoliberal regulation of social work practice and education. *Alternative Routes, 26*, 251–276.

Mandell, D. (Ed.) (2007). *Revisiting the use of self in social work: Questioning professional identities.* Toronto: Canadian Scholars' Press.

Mandell, D. (2008). Power, care and vulnerability: Considering use of self in child welfare work. *Journal of Social Work Practice, 22*(2), 235–248.

Mandell, D., & Hundert, A. (2015). Social justice and social work: Convergence and divergence in the wake of the Toronto G20 Summit. In N. Yu & D. Mandell (Eds.), *Subversive action: Extralegal practices for social justice.* Waterloo, Ontario: Wilfrid University Press.

Margaroni, M. (2007). Recent work on and by Julia Kristeva: Toward a psychoanalytic social theory. *Signs, 32*(3), 793–808.

Martinez-Brawley, E. (2001). Searching again and again: Inclusion, hetero-geneity and social work research. *British Journal of Social Work, 31*(2), 271–285.

Martinez-Brawley, E., & Zorita, P. M. (2007). Tacit and codified knowl-edge in social work: A critique of standardization in education and prac-tice. *Families in Society, 88*(4), 534–542.

Massumi, B. (2002). *Parables for the virtual: Movement, affect, sensation.* Minneapolis: University of Minnesota Press.

McGrath, S., Lee, B., Moffatt, K., Carranza, M., & Lagios, A. (2015). Col-lective trauma as a personal/social concern for LGBTTTSQ persons. In B. O'Neill, T. Swan, & N. Mule (Eds.), *LGBTQ people and social work: Intersectional perspectives* (pp. 213–232). Toronto: Canadian Scholars' Press.

Miehls, D., & Moffatt, K. (2000). Constructing social work identity based on reflexive self. *British Journal of Social Work, 30*(3), 339–348.

Moffatt, K. (1999a). The surveillance and governance of the welfare recipi-ent. In A. Chambon, A. Irving, & L. Epstein (Eds.), *Reading Foucault for social work* (pp. 219–245). New York: Columbia University Press.

Moffatt, K. (1999b). Teaching social work practice as a reflective process. In N. Gould & I. Taylor (Eds.), *Reflective learning for social work: Research, theory and practice* (pp. 47–61). Aldershot, UK: Ashgate.

Moffatt, K. (2001a). *A poetics of social work: Personal agency and social trans-formation in Canada, 1920–1939.* Toronto: University of Toronto Press.

Moffatt, K. (2001b). Reconsidering reflection in the postcolonial classroom. In S. Steinberg (Ed.), *Multi/intercultural conversations: A reader* (pp. 287–300). New York: Peter Lang.

Moffatt, K. (2004). Beyond male denial and female shame: Learning about gender in sociocultural concepts class. *Smith College Studies in Social Work, 74*(2), 243–256.

Moffatt, K. (2006). Grading as the coding of student desire in the context of lacking. *Radical Pedagogy 8*(2). Retrieved from http://radicalpedagogy .icaap.org/content/issue8_2/moffatt.html

Moffatt, K. (2012a). Dancing without a floor: The artists' politic of queer club space. In K. Moffatt (Ed.), *Troubled masculinities: Reimag-ining urban men* (pp. 127–142). Toronto: University of Toronto Press.

Moffatt, K. (2012b). Instruction in the art of the masculine: The art of Daryl Vocat. In K. Moffatt (Ed.), *Troubled masculinities: Reimagining urban men* (pp. 6–76). Toronto: University of Toronto Press.

Moffatt, K. (2012c). Introduction. In K. Moffatt (Ed.), *Troubled masculinities: Reimagining urban men* (pp. 3–20). Toronto: University of Toronto Press.

Moffatt, K. (2012d, Summer). Shame and men: A queer perspective on masculinity. *C Magazine, 114*, 5–8.

Moffatt, K. (Ed.) (2012e). *Troubled masculinities: Reimagining urban men.* Toronto: University of Toronto Press.

Moffatt, K. (2017, May). Arts-inspired social work research. In *Health and societies: Interdisciplinary thinking within interethnic contexts.* Symposium conducted by Ryerson University and Université Denis Diderot (Paris), Toronto.

Moffatt, K., Carranza, M., Lee, B., McGrath, S., & George, U. (2012). Collective trauma as a personal/social concern for persons within marginalized communities. *International Journal of Community Diversity, 12*(4), 61–80.

Moffatt, K., George, P., Alphonse, M., Kanitkar, A., Anand, V., & Chamberlain, J. (2009). Community practice at a crossroads: The impact of the global on the local in India. *Community Development Journal, 44*(4), 1–18.

Moffatt, K., George, U., Lee, B., & McGrath, S. (2005). Community practice researchers as reflective learners. *British Journal of Social Work, 35*(1), 89–104.

Moffatt, K., & Miehls, D. (1999). Development of student identity: Evolution from neutrality to subjectivity. *Journal of Teaching in Social Work, 19*(1–2), 65–76.

Moffatt, K., Panitch, M., Parada, H., Todd, S., Barnoff, L., & Aslett, J. (2016). "Essential cogs in the innovation machine": The discourse of innovation in Ontario educational reform. *Review of Education, Pedagogy and Cultural Studies, 38*(4), 317–340.

Moffatt, K., Todd, S., Barnoff, L., Pyne, J., Panitch, M., Parada, H., . . . Hunter-Young, N. (2018). Worry about professional education: Emotions and affect in the context of neoliberal change in postsecondary education. *Emotions, Space and Society, 26*, 9–15.

Morley, C. (2014). Using critical reflection to research possibilities for change. *British Journal of Social Work, 44*, 1419–1435.

Mountz, A., Bounds, A., Mansfield, B., Lloyd, J., Hyndman, J., Walton-Roberts, M., . . . Curran W. (2015). For slow scholarship: A feminist politics of resistance through collective action in the neoliberal university. *ACME: An International Educational Journal of Critical Geography, 14*(4), 1235–1259.

Mullaly, R. (2007). *The new structural social work* (3rd ed.). Don Mills, Ontario: Oxford University Press.

Munt, S. (2008). *Queer attachments: The cultural politics of shame*. Aldershot, UK: Ashgate.

Napier, L., & Fook, J. (2000). Reflective practice in social work. In L. Napier & J. Fook (Eds.), *Breakthroughs in practice: Theorising critical moments in social work* (pp. 1–15). London: Whiting and Birch.

Narayan, L. (2000). Freire and Gandhi: Their relevance for social work education. *International Social Work, 43*(2), 193–204.

Nelson, S. (2012). The lost path to emancipatory practice: Towards a history of reflective practice in nursing. *Nursing Philosophy, 13,* 202–213.

Nicholls, P. (1991). Divergences: Modernism, postmodernism, Jameson and Lyotard. *Critical Quarterly, 33*(3), 1–18.

Oliver, K. (2002). Introduction: Kristeva's revolutions. In K. Oliver (Ed.), *The portable Kristeva* (pp. xi–ix). New York: Columbia University Press.

Orcutt, B. E. (1990). *Science and inquiry in social work practice.* New York: Columbia University Press.

Parada, H., Barnoff, L., Moffatt, K., & Homan, M. (2010). *Promoting community change: Making it happen in the real world.* Toronto: Thomson.

Participatory Geographies Research Group. (2012). Connectivity, creativity, hope and fuller subjectivities: Appreciating responses to the communifesto for fuller geographies. Retrieved from http://radicalantipode .files.wordpress.com/2012/12/pygyrg-reply.pdf

Parton, N. (2009). Postmodern and constructionist approaches to social work. In R. Adams, L. Dominelli, & M. Payne (Eds.), *Critical practice in social work* (2nd ed.) (pp. 220–229). New York: Palgrave Macmillan.

Paton, C. (2015). Bringing relating to the forefront: Using the art of improvisation to perceive relational processes actively in social work. In

C. Sinding & H. Barnes (Eds.), *Social work artfully: Beyond borders and boundaries* (pp. 191–204). Waterloo, Ontario: Wilfred Laurier Press.

Paulo Freire biography. (n.d.). Retrieved from http://www.freire.org/paulo -freire/paulo-freire-biography

Pease, B. (1999). Deconstructing masculinity—reconstructing men. In B. Pease & J. Fook (Eds.), *Transforming social work practice: Postmodern critical perspectives* (pp. 97–120). New York: Routledge.

Pease, B. (2002). Rethinking empowerment: A postmodern reappraisal for emancipatory practice. *British Journal of Social Work, 32*, 135–147.

Pease, B., & Fook, J. (1999). Postmodern critical theory and emancipatory social work practice. In B. Pease & J. Fook (Eds.), *Transforming social work practice: Postmodern critical perspectives* (pp. 1–24). New York: Routledge.

Peters, M., & Besley, T. (2008). Academic entrepreneurship and the creative economy. *Thesis Eleven, 94*, 88–105.

Phillips, C. (2007). Untitled moments: Theorizing incorporeal knowledge in social work practice. *Qualitative Social Work, 6*(4), 447–464.

Pietroni, M. (1995). The nature and aims of professional education for social workers: A postmodern perspective. In M. Yelloly & M. Henkel (Eds.), *Learning and teaching in social work: Towards reflective practice* (pp. 34–50) London: Jessica Kingsley.

Pollack, S., & Rossiter, A. (2010). Neoliberalism and the entrepreneurial subject: Implications for feminism and social work. *Canadian Social Work Review, 27*(2), 155–169.

Pon, G. (2009). Cultural competence as a new racism: An ontology of for- getting. *Journal of Progressive Human Services, 20*, 59–71.

Pon, G., Gosine, K., & Phillips, D. (2011). Immediate response: Address- ing anti-Native and anti-Black racism in child welfare. *International Journal of Child, Youth and Family Studies, 2*(3/4), 385–409.

Preston, S., & Aslett, J. (2014). Resisting neoliberalism from within the academy: Subversion through an activist pedagogy. *Social Work Educa- tion, 33*(4), 502–518.

Pyne, J. (2016). Queer and trans collisions in the classroom: A call to throw open theoretical doors in social work education. In S. Hillock & N. Mule (Eds.), *Queering social work education* (pp. 54–72). Vancouver, B.C.: UBC Press.

Rose, N. (1999). *Powers of freedom: Reframing political thought.* Cambridge: Cambridge University Press.

Rose, N., O'Malley, P., & Valverde, M. (2006). Governmentality. *Annual Review of Law and Social Science, 2*, 83–104.

Rossiter, A. (2000). The professional is political: An interpretation of the problem of the past in solution-focused therapy. *American Journal of Orthopsychiatry, 70*(2), 151–160.

Roy, K. (2005). Power and resistance: Insurgent spaces, Deleuze and curriculum, *Journal of Curriculum Theorizing 21* (1), 27–38.

Rwomire, A., & Radithokwa, L. (1996). Social work in Africa: Issues and challenges. *Journal of Social Development in Africa, 11*(2), 5–19.

Saleebey, D. (2013). *The strengths perspective in social work practice* (6th ed.). Boston: Pearson.

Schön, D. (1983). *The reflective practitioner.* New York: Basic Books.

Schön, D. (1987). *Educating the reflective practitioner.* San Francisco: Jossey-Bass.

Schön, D. (1992). The theory of inquiry: Dewey's legacy to education. *Curriculum Inquiry, 22*(2), 119–139.

Schroeder, W. (2005). *Continental philosophy: A critical approach.* Malden, Mass.: Blackwell.

Scott, D., & Usher, R. (2011). *Researching education: Data, methods and theory in educational enquiry.* New York: Continuum.

Sedgwick, E. (2003). *Touching feeling: Affect, pedagogy, performativity.* Durham, N.C.: Duke University Press.

Sedgwick, E., & Frank, A. (1995). Shame in the cybernetic fold: Reading Silvan Tomkins. *Critical Inquiry, 21*(2), 496–522.

Sewpaul, V. (2006). The global–local dialectic: Challenges for African scholarship and social work in a post-colonial world. *British Journal of Social Work, 36*(3), 419–434.

Shore, M. (1987). *The science of social redemption: McGill, the Chicago School and the origins of social research in Canada.* Toronto: University of Toronto Press.

Sinding, C., & Barnes, H. (Eds.). (2015). *Social work artfully: Beyond borders and boundaries.* Waterloo, Ontario: Wilfred Laurier Press.

Sirotich, F., Martin, S., Ruhinda, S., Vaz, J., & Moffatt, K. (2012). Yearning to break the silence: Reflections on the function of male silence. In

K. Moffatt (Ed.), *Troubled masculinities: Reimagining urban men* (pp. 42–60). Toronto: University of Toronto Press.

Smith, A. (1997). The limits of communication: Lyotard and Levinas on otherness. In M. Huspek & G. Radford (Eds.), *Transgressing discourses: Communication and the voice of the other* (pp. 329–353). Albany: State University of New York Press.

Smith, K. (2007). Social work, restructuring and everyday resistance: "Best practices" gone underground. In D. Baines (Ed.), *Doing anti-oppressive practice: Building transformative politicized social work* (pp. 148–159). Halifax, Nova Scotia: Fernwood.

Stern, M. (2012). "We can't build our dreams on suspicious minds": Neoliberalism, education policy and the feelings left over. *Culture Studies Critical Methodologies, 12*(5), 387–400.

Tanke, J. J. (2009). *Foucault's philosophy of art: A genealogy of modernity.* New York: Continuum.

Tejaswini, P., & Ennis, G. M. (2018). Critically reflecting on the Australian Association of Social Workers Code of Ethics: Learning from a social work field placement. *British Journal of Social Work, 48*, 1370–1387.

Thien, D. (2005). After or beyond feeling? A consideration of affect and emotion in geography. *Area, 37*(4), 450–454.

Todd, S. (2005). Unfinished fictions: Becoming and unbecoming a feminist community organizers. In S. Hick, J. Fook, & R. Puzzuto (Eds.), *Social work: A critical turn* (pp. 137–152). Toronto: Thompson.

Todd, S. (2007). Post-structural possibilities: Beyond structural practice in child protection. *Canadian Social Work Review, 24*(1), 23–37.

Todd, S. (2012). Practicing in the uncertain: Reworking standardized clients as improv theatre. *Social Work Education, 31*(3), 302–315.

Todd, S., Barnoff, L., Moffatt, K., Panitch, M., Parada, H., Mucina, M., & Williams, D. (2015). Performativity culture in universities: Social work fabrications. *British Journal of Social Work, 45*(2), 511–526.

Todd, S., Barnoff, L., Moffatt, K., Panitch, M., Parada, H., & Strumm, B. (2017). A social work re-reading of students as consumers. *Social Work Education, 36*(5), 542–556.

Todd, S., & Schwartz, K. (2009). Thinking through quality in field education: Integrating alternative and traditional learning opportunities. *Social Work Education, 28*(4), 380–395.

Trevelyan, C., Crath, R., & Chambon, A. (2012). Promoting critical reflexivity through arts-based media: A case study. *British Journal of Social Work, 44,* 7–26.

Turk, J. (Ed.). (2000). *The corporate campus: Commercialization and the dangers to Canada's colleges and universities.* Toronto: Lorimer.

Turk, J. (2008a). Restructuring academic work. In J. Turk (Ed.), *Universities at risk: How politics, special interests and corporatization threaten academic integrity.* Toronto: Lorimer.

Turk, J. (Ed.). (2008b). *Universities at risk: How politics, special interests and corporatization threaten academic integrity.* Toronto: Lorimer.

Ungar, M. (2004). Surviving as a postmodern social worker: Two Ps and three Rs of direct practice. *Social Work, 49*(3), 489–496.

Valverde, M. (1991). *The age of light, soap, and water: Moral reform in English Canada, 1885–1925.* Toronto: McClelland and Stewart.

Wagner, A., & Yee, J. Y. (2011). Anti-oppression in higher education: Implicating neoliberalism. *Canadian Social Work Review, 28* (1), 89–105.

Wang, F. (1999). Resistance and old age: The subject behind the American seniors' movement. In A. Chambon, A. Irving, & L. Epstein (Eds.), *Reading Foucault for social work* (pp. 189–219). New York: Columbia University Press.

Wehbi, S. (2015). Arts-informed teaching practice: Examples from a graduate anti-oppression class. *Social Work Education, 34*(1), 46–59.

Wehbi, S., El-Lahib, Y., Perreault-Laird, J., & Zakharova, G. (2018). Oasis in a concrete jungle: Arts-informed methods in social work classrooms. *Social Work Education, 37*(5), 617–632.

Wehbi, S., McCormick, K., & Angelucci, S. (2016). Socially engaged art and social work: Reflecting on an interdisciplinary course development. *Journal of Progressive Human Services, 27*(1), 49–64.

Wehbi, S., Preston, S., & Moffatt, K. (2016). Introducing art into the social work classroom: Tensions and possibilities. In J. Gingras, P. Robinson, J. Waddell, & J. Cooper (Eds.), *Teaching as scholarship: Preparing students for professional practice in community services* (pp. 155–176). Waterloo, Ontario: Wilfrid Laurier Press.

Wersun, A. (2010). Triple translation: Academic and managerial discourses of knowledge transfer policy in a new university in Scotland. *Discourse: Studies in the Cultural Politics of Education, 31*(5), 665–682.

Wikipedia: About. (2018, December 29). Retrieved from https://en.wikipedia.org/wiki/Wikipedia:About

Wikipedia: Five Pillars. (2018, November 17). Retrieved from https://en.wikipedia.org/wiki/Wikipedia:Five_pillars

Willson, R. (2018). *A guide for the idealist: Launching and navigating your planning career.* New York: Routledge.

Wilson, C., Oliver, V., Flicker, S., Native Youth Sexual Health Network, Prentice, T., Jackson, R., . . . Mitchell, C. (2016). "Culture" as HIV prevention: Indigenous youth speak up! *Gateways: International Journal of Community Research and Engagement, 9*(1), 74–88.

Witkin, S. (2012a). An introduction to social construction. In S. Witkin (Ed.), *Social construction and social work practice* (pp. 13–37). New York: Columbia University Press.

Witkin, S. (Ed.). (2012b). *Social construction and social work practice.* New York: Columbia University Press.

Witkin, S. (2014a). Autoethnography: The opening act. In S. Witkin (Ed.), *Narrating social work through autoethnography* (pp. 1–24). New York: Columbia University Press.

Witkin S. (Ed.) (2014b). *Narrating social work through autoethnography.* New York: Columbia University Press.

Witkin, S. (2017). *Transforming social work: Social constructionist reflections on contemporary and enduring issues.* London: Palgrave.

Wojnarowicz, D. (2018). *The weight of the earth: The tape journals of David Wojnarowicz* (L. Darms & D. O'Neill, Eds.). Los Angeles: Semiotext(e).

Woodhouse, H. (2009). *Selling out: Academic freedom and the corporate market.* Montreal: McGill-Queens University Press

Yee, J., & Dumbrill, G. (2003). Whiteout: Looking for race in Canadian social work practice. In J. Graham & A. Al-Krenawi (Eds.), *Canadian social work practice* (pp. 98–121). Don Mills, UK : Oxford University Press.

Yee, J. Y., & Wagner, A. (2013). Is anti-oppression teaching in Canadian social work classrooms a form of neo-liberalism? *Social Work Education, 32*(3), 331–348.

Youdell, D., & Armstrong, F. (2011). A politics beyond subjects: The affective choreographies and smooth spaces of schooling. *Emotion, Space and Society, 4*, 144–150.

Youdell, D., & McGimpsey, I. (2015). Assembling, disassembling, and reassembling youth services in Austerity Britain. *Critical Studies in Education, 56*(1), 116–130.

INDEX

GPSR Authorized Representative: Easy Access System Europe, Mustamäe tee 50, 10621 Tallinn, Estonia, gpsr.requests@easproject.com